ALEPH CLASSICS

THE TIRUKKURAL

The Indian subcontinent's literary heritage is unparalleled. For thousands of years significant literary works have been created in many languages—Sanskrit, Tamil, Prakrit, Pali, Urdu and Persian to name a few. Aleph Classics is committed to publishing new translations of the most significant of these works from time to time. These translations will be aimed squarely at the twenty-first-century reader—they will be distinguished by their readability, accessibility and scholarship. Aleph Classics will be elegantly laid out, designed and printed, and will carry on the company's tradition of publishing handsome, enduring books.

Books by Gopalkrishna Gandhi

FICTION
Refuge

NON-FICTION
Of a Certain Age: Twenty Life Sketches

PLAYS
Dara Shukoh: A Play

TRANSLATIONS
Koi Achha Sa Ladka
(Translation of *A Suitable Boy* by Vikram Seth into Hindustani)

BOOKS EDITED BY GOPALKRISHNA GANDHI

Gandhi and South Africa (with E. S. Reddy)
Gandhi and Sri Lanka
Nehru and Sri Lanka
India House, Colombo: Portrait of a Residence
Gandhi Is Gone: Who Will Guide Us Now?
A Frank Friendship: Gandhi and Bengal: A Descriptive Chronology
The Oxford India Gandhi: Essential Writings
My Dear Bapu: Letters from C. Rajagopalachari to Mohandas Karamchand Gandhi

TIRUVALLUVAR

THE
TIRUKKURAL

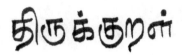

திருக்குறள்

A New English Version by

GOPALKRISHNA GANDHI

ALEPH

ALEPH

ALEPH BOOK COMPANY
An independent publishing firm
promoted by *Rupa Publications India*

Published in India in 2015 by
Aleph Book Company
7/16 Ansari Road, Daryaganj
New Delhi 110 002

ISBN: 978-93-83064-70-0

9 10

Printed at Sanat Printers

To the conflicted yet interwoven memories of
Chakravarti Rajagopalachari
(1878–1972)
and
Periyar E. V. Ramasami
(1879–1973)

Men of the light are men who care
Their words humane, hard messages bear
Tirukkural, Verse 91

CONTENTS

PREFACE
THE TIRUKKURAL

I

For the many who know the *Tirukkural*, this initial word about the book will be redundant. For those unfamiliar with Tiruvalluvar's undimming work, a brief description of it might be useful.

Both the author's name and that of the work are 'given', that is, they are not original names, for we do not know what he was actually called, and he did not title his work.

'Kural' in Tamil means 'short'. The 1,330 couplets that make up the *Tirukkural* are short, each making a compact, concise proposition. The first line, typically, has four words, the second has three. The syllables per line can sometimes vary, but not the number of words or metrical feet. Together, they are like a cluster of seven gems, set in two rows. The *Tirukkural*—'the honoured *Kural*'—is traditionally dated to the immediate post-Sangam period, referring to the era of the Tamil academies (sangams) that are said to have flourished between 300 BCE and 300 CE. The *Kural* deploys the austerity of the Venba metrical form with its ellipses (tohai) to telling effect. Its author uses metrical feet (cir), alliteration (monai), second-letter alliteration (ethuhai) and rhythm (osai) like a master of cryptograms. Verbs are absent, nouns truant. This economy tightens the expression to that point beyond which tightening would strangle meaning. The opening couplet offers a perfect sample:

Akara mudala ezhutellam adi
Bhagavan mudatre ulahu

The first word of each line clicks into an internal rhyme + alliteration with the correspondence of sounds occurring without variation in the second letter before the rhythm flows into the third: A-**ka**ra/ Bha-**ga**va(n). Sanskrit has borrowed this as 'dvitakshara prasa' (alliteration in the second letter). 'Containing', in the words of the book's best-known translator, G. U. Pope, 'a complete and striking idea expressed in a refined metre', every one of the 1,330 kurals is believed to be the work of a single author, Tiruvalluvar. Written sometime between 2 BCE and 5 CE, the *Tirukkural* speaks within a frame, thinks without frontiers. It is presented in three Books. The first has traditionally been called the Book of Virtue, the second the Book of Wealth, the third the Book of Love. They deal with, respectively, righteous living, statecraft and conjugal love.

Tiruvalluvar was an exceptionally powerful thinker, a master of his language and its literature's complex poetic forms. He was a sharp observer of life. The *Kural* is the result of his literary labours, a spectacular insight into the workings of the human brain and the waywardness of the human heart. Admired as literature, venerated as secular gospel, translated times without number into the world's different languages, the *Tirukkural*'s teachings have yet been ignored by generation after generation of an unwise humanity.

II

When smitten by a book, readers want to become part of it, immerse themselves in the life of the volume they hold in their hands.

While the fever is on, they cannot part with the book. They keep it on their person, as W. B. Yeats did his copy of Tagore's *Gitanjali*. 'I have carried the manuscript of these translations about with me for days, reading it in railway trains, or on the top of omnibuses and in restaurants, and I have often had to close it lest some stranger would see how much it moved me.'

They of course talk about it as of a personal, even private, discovery to those close to them. Some of them, if they think of themselves as writers, will try to find a journal that might carry their review of it. The most ambitious, even audacious, way of finding a union with the work—for that is what the smitten want—is to try translating it and thereby enter the work's very soul.

'Translator ambition' includes new translations in the same language and, in the case of fiction, screen versions and film scripts. Given in generosity, the permission is often regretted in hindsight. R. K. Narayan recounts how his novel, *The Guide,* when it was made into a film became another being. The location, he was told, need not be where he had visualized it to be. 'Malgudi will be where we place it, in Kashmir, Rajasthan, Bombay, Delhi, even Ceylon.'

When he protested that a tiger fight scene would be wrong, for there was no such thing in the story, he was assured that it was. He just gave up, in the spirit of the first line of a song in that film sung by Mohammed Rafi—'Kya se kya ho gaya!' meaning 'What have you gone and done!'

An author may dearly wish the go-ahead had not been given to a translator or to that mutilator calling himself 'transcreator', bemoan the translation's excesses and lament its shortfalls, but once the deed is done, the translator becomes, for all time, part of the work's aura.

Not all translations, of course, come about that way. Some are commissioned by the author or a publisher quite matter-of-factly for the benefit of readers belonging to another linguistic register. For the 'engaged' translator such exercises can be no less fulfilling—or self-fulfilling—than for the self-appointed one. This translation of Tiruvalluvar's 1,330 rhymed Tamil aphorisms belongs to the latter category. It could very well make Valluvar exclaim from his post-earthly world: 'What have you gone and done!'

When David Davidar asked me if I would consider translating the *Tirukkural* into English, I was, to say the least, startled. Trying to imagine myself doing this, I said: 'I do speak the kind of "home Tamil" those descended from a Tamil household do, and the only Tamil reading I have done is of newspapers. And as for the *Kural*, I have read it only in Rajagopalachari's English translation—that's all.' Exactly for that reason, David went on to say, a new version in modern, accessible English was worth placing in the hands of a new generation of readers, especially those not familiar with Tamil. 'In any case, between the rendering by Rajaji done in the 1930s and one that might be attempted eighty and more years later, several decades have passed.' And then, mining his own knowledge of the text, said: 'Many of us whose mother tongue is Tamil have known the couplet: "Karka kasadara karpavai kattrapin / nirka adharku thaga"...and have known it to mean, generally, "Learn whatever you learn thoroughly, without doubts or defects, and then apply the learning", but the saying needs to be refreshed now for our times.'

'Let me,' I said, 'first take a close look at the text.'

♦

Rumination preceded reading. I recalled four occasions when the *Kural* was cited to me in the ordinary course of things. I was not yet twenty when I heard Rajagopalachari describe the speed of the assistance rushed by officers to flood victims in the Krishna and Godavari basins in 1954. He was chief minister of undivided Madras at that time. 'How would you describe,' he asked me, 'the speed of help that comes the very moment it is needed?'

'The speed of light?'

'Yes...but Tiruvalluvar has a better description for that speed. He describes it in his great work that you must read one day, called the *Kural*, as the speed of the hand that moves the very instant a garment slips, to halt its fall...'

It was some years later that I read his rendering of the 788th kural in which, to the description of the slipping garment, he adds, typical of his conservatism, a context: 'slips in company'. Every translator adds something, be it ever so slight, to the original.

My second recollection is of 1969. I was an IAS Probationer in Tanjore when the young but unbelievably wise sub-collector of Kumbakonam, D. Murugaraj told me: 'The Gita is a great book, but the Kural, in my view, ranks higher. Whatever else you read as a trainee in Tamil Nadu, you have to read that masterpiece.'

A couple of years later, at the inauguration of a school near Gingee, where I was posted as an assistant collector, an MLA was pontificating on the virtues of learning. 'Men of learning,' he quoted from the book, 'have eyes, blockheads have two sores.' The 393rd kural seemed to have been tailor-made for the man himself but I let my wicked thought pass.

My fourth induction into the *Kural* being invoked is from a decade later. Watching me entranced by my two little daughters' baby talk, my mother said, 'You know, the *Kural* says those who call the veena's sound or the taste of honey sweet have not heard their own little one's sweet lisps...' Her words came fluting into my mind as I now read the 66th kural. It was with these random recollections refreshed in my thoughts that I opened, for the first time in my life, the 1,330 kurals. I found that I just could not make out their meaning. It is an unusual experience to be able to read a script but not get the sense of what you are reading. Of each couplet—with four words or feet in the first line, three in the second—I could just about understand one or two. Five or six—the majority—of the words were completely beyond my comprehension. And this is where my obtaining the Rev. G. U. Pope 1886 English translation made all the difference. Rukmini Devi Arundale's collection of antiquarian books in Kalakshetra, Chennai, has a 1980 reprint of Pope's translation entitled *The Sacred Kurral*, giving the author's name as 'Tiruvalluva-Nayanar'. This particular reproduction by Asian Educational Services, New Delhi, is only thirty-five years old but has already browned into the feel of an old book. Its pages melt and come off when turned. Poring over them as gingerly as I could, I could see why Pope's English rendition of the *Kural* is regarded as definitive.

Pope has gone into the work like a conch fisher dives into the sea. He disappears into the *Kural* to emerge with a find that is from that point on 'his'. He gives us a Valluvar that is his Valluvar, a *Kural* that is his *Kural* and yet is unmistakably Valluvar's. Reading Pope's renderings, matching them with the Tamil verses and then dipping into Beschi's Latin equivalent (1730) and the rephrasings of F. W. Ellis, both of which Pope appends to his volume, was sheer exhilaration.

The Lexicon and Concordance given at the end of his work proved invaluable. In his translation, Pope gives us his understanding of the couplets; in the Lexicon and Concordance he gives us the word-to-word meaning as if saying 'Check my version out, word by word'. Going back and forth in this study, I knew I was 'caught' and the originator of Aleph Book Company was not surprised. David Davidar knew the classic's timeless appeal. And before I quite realized it, I found myself becoming a 'commissioned translator' of the work and, exactly like the besotted reader, entering its deathless life.

I also returned, as I had to, to the much-thumbed copy of Bharatiya Vidya Bhavan's 1965 edition of Rajagopalachari's translation and commentary in our home's peripatetic bookshelves. Half a century old, its binding had all but come apart. But on my picking it up now it 'held' in more senses than one. Rajagopalachari calls this edition of his translation, rather didactically, *Kural: The Great Book of Tiru-Valluvar*. Very different from his much more interesting Rochouse title (*The Second Book of Kural: A Selection from the Old Tamil Code for Princes, Statesmen and Men of Affairs*). I then noticed something all *Kural* experts know but that I had missed all these decades. Like Beschi, the moralist in Rajagopalachari not only leaves out Book III (the Book of Love) from his attention, he draws a veil over its very existence.

Domestic censorship is the surest allurement to a 'home kid' and so as a grandson, albeit nudging seventy, of the veiler, I had to turn to Book III in Pope's version like to forbidden fruit. Valluvar is not Vatsyayana but there is in the frequently vanishing seaman longed for by the woman a figure of curious sensuality. The reader may see what I mean in the translation.

Given Valluvar's mastery of sea lore, I could not help but wonder at the goddess of coincidences who steered me to the doors of a lighthouse-maker for my initiation into the *Kural*. The *Kural*-smitten neighbour in my suburb of Chennai, a retired deputy director general of Lighthouses and Lightships, K. N. Varadarajan, told me of other translations and commentaries, adding his own fascinating comments.

A foundational fortune came by way of a conversation with the Chennai-based historian and scholar of classical and modern Tamil, Professor A. R. Venkatachalapathy (Chala). Understanding my enthusiasm and my diffidence, Chala said I absolutely must have some working sessions with a friend of his he described as a person of remarkable scholarship and equally remarkable modesty, the Tiruchirappalli-based scholar and professor of Tamil, B. Mathivanan. Meeting Mathi was an education. I have not seen anyone wear scholarship as lightly as he does. Mathi showed me the inestimable value of several couplets without raising them to the status of Mosaic tablets. He touched them with a feather, as if only dusting them, to help me see what they held. Chala and Mathi spared several hours for me, leading me, cross-textually, to read Valluvar through Parimelazhagar and Pope, with Tamizhannal's commentaries on the Valluvar original. The very simplified renderings in Tamil by Sujata (*Tirukkural: Puthiya Urai*, 1995) the simplifier of voting technology in the shape of the electronic voting machine and those done into economical English by P. S. Sundaram (*The Tirukkural*, 1991) were most useful to me.

◆

I need to tell my reader how I have engaged with the task.

This is not what might be called 'a new translation', for its point of departure is not Valluvar's original in Sangam Tamil but Pope's rendering of it in Victorian English. I have tried to render it in the English of our globalized times.

Put simply, I am sharing with readers what I have read into each couplet of Valluvar's through Pope's magnifying glass. Lighting that lucent disc with my own 'cell-torch', I am interpreting each couplet, at second, third remove. My interpretations are in the spoken English of our times. 'Thee' and 'thou' have yielded to 'you' and 'our'. And in has come the Valluvar 'I'.

Valluvar does not use the first person singular, but in each couplet one can hear his speaking voice. 'Take it from me', he seems to say, in ever so many of the couplets, 'believe me', in many others. He talks through them as to a person sitting beside him, one on one. I have sought to increase the timbre of Valluvar's conversational voice as distinct from his tutorial voice.

Can words in a line have a stance, a couplet something like a posture? I believe they can. We carry two visual images of Valluvar reinforced in our minds by the stone, bronze and plaster statues of his presumed likeness. The first, and most prevalent, is of him seated cross-legged on the floor, stylus in hand. The second, given to us by the monumental stone image at Kanyakumari, has him standing. In both he is an imposing figure, literally and metaphorically an elevated personality, a teacher-figure, evoking respect and awe. So impactful have the statues been on our thinking, on our view of the world and of life itself that we find a certain contentment, even fulfilment, in seeing him on a pedestal. This compacts the power of his word with the strength of his image.

But the pedestalling also widens the acoustic space between him and us. Valluvar seated high is Valluvar given respect. But Valluvar seated high also distances Valluvar. It obscures the *Kural*'s author who converses rather than pronounces, discusses rather than prescribes. And so, supplementing Valluvar's pedagogical stance or posture, I have tried to see in his couplets a Valluvar who relaxes his voice's pitch, uncrosses his legs, and takes us by the hand from his formal plinth or pedestal to his home's pyol or thinnai, the seat built into its outer veranda where the stranger and the friend may both find an equal welcome.

It is time a new generation of international readers gets to hear Valluvar in an English it is at home in. A contemporary English rendering of Valluvar would need to be direct, conversational. It would need to be spoken, not declaimed. It would need to be communicated person to person, on the same level, not intoned from a height to one down below. Pope's rhymed English version stays solid. It needs freshening, refreshening in an English this century knows, to find its Valluvar anew. And this is what is attempted here—in the doing flawed, in spirit true.

That the exercise should be in verse was clear to me from the start. Valluvar has written the *Kural* in verse, a translation of the *Kural* should ideally be in verse. Else, it will be a commentary. But why I have attempted that translation in rhymed verse, I cannot really say, for I do not quite know the reason myself. One reason could be that since Pope has done it that way and as I am offering Valluvar through Pope, my renderings should adhere to the form Pope has used. The Venba metre is not to be replicated in English, but a rendering in verse should have some semblance of rhyme, metre and rhythm.

With three couplets—481, 774 and 801—I have taken the liberty of stretching the rendering to well beyond two lines. Each *Kural* couplet has been condensed by Valluvar into a tight knot beyond which it cannot be further reduced. Several dimensions of it are coiled into its seven words in what can only be called a marvel of mineral compaction. It is possible to—indeed, one may say Valluvar expects a reader to—open each couplet up, reveal all its compressed dimensions. I have attempted precisely this with these three couplets and a few others to show as a sample how much meaning, how much imagery, is contained within the couplet's strict compass and how that can be unravelled.

No translation of Valluvar has been, can be or will be the last. Each generation will have not just one but several reinterpretations of the *Kural* that could well be improvements, in fidelity and form, in expression and elucidation. This, therefore, is only an addition to the self-renewing series of *Kural* translations, each of which will angle a new light on that immortal work, catching perchance a facet of its wisdom more sharply than others while being sure to miss another. Or will adjust listener-acoustics so as to hear one note more clearly than others, while surely losing another.

And so, offered here, with reverence to Valluvar's translators and commentators, old, recent and those yet to come, is yet another interpretation in an English the twenty-first century might be happier with as a medium of its conversation with the nameless and ageless Wise One.

July 2015

Gopalkrishna Gandhi
Chennai

INTRODUCTION

Hunting tiger in the summer of 1810, an officer of the 28th Cavalry rode into the tangle of forest that had covered the caves at Ajanta for centuries. One does not know what he made of the frescoes he saw in those dark recesses, but John Smith sought at once to become one with them. He carved his name right across a painted Bodhisattva. That was crass and yet, were it not for the tiger-thirsty cavalryman, these masterpieces of Buddhist art with depictions of the life of the Buddha and vignettes from the Jataka tales would have remained known only to people living in the caves' vicinity for another century. Archaeological science has, in the years since John Smith, enabled us to know that these thirty rock-cut Buddhist cave monuments date from anywhere between 2 BCE to about 480 or 650 CE.

SEALED ART

Seven to eight hundred years is a long span of supposition for dating a work of art. But when sharper focus eludes us, it is wise to widen rather than narrow the window of probability. Around the same broad frame of time that the Ajanta frescoes were being created by unknown painters, it is likely that Tiruvalluvar was at work on his masterpiece of couplets, collectively known as the *Tirukkural*.

I say likely because, as I have said in the preface, those two names of author and book, respectively, are assigned names, assigned by respect and awe; we do not know the original ones.

The *Kural*'s French translator, M. Ariel, has said famously about the work: 'Ce livre sans nom, par un auteur sans nom (A book without a name by an author without a name).' But those two names have been used now for centuries, by popular endorsement and acclaim. The name 'Tiruvalluvar' first occurs in the tenth century in a text called *Tiruvalluvamaalai*. Believed by some to have lived between 2 BCE and 5 CE and by others, much later, between 1 CE and 8 CE, somewhere in the coastal town of what is now Mylapore, in Madras or Chennai, Tiruvalluvar and his work remained sealed to all but his Tamil-speaking admirers for close to a millennium. Five (according to some, ten) ancient commentators on Tiruvalluvar's work, with dated and perfectly matching texts, have been the pillars of the *Kural*. For over a millennium now, the *Kural* has been known only as we know it today; no other recension of it has changed or challenged the sway of that one integral, text—a remarkable achievement that stamps it with both antiquity and authenticity. Of its commentators, Parimelazhagar (13 CE) is the most important. To Valluvar's Socrates, Parimelazhagar is Plato, except that in Valluvar's case, the original words come ringing in directly from the author himself. Parimelazhagar comments on them; he does not have to construct or re-construct them. The *Kural* text that his commentary has used has been accepted without a contrary view or version as part of the rich didactic literature emerging in the immediate post-Sangam period (circa 300 BCE to 300 CE).

AN ITALIAN OPENS IT TO THE WORLD
Known and cherished in lonely learning by the world of Tamil letters, this nugget of 1,330 couplets remained invisible to the outside world until about eighty years before Smith's historic stumble into ancient art, when an Italian Jesuit serving in the Madurai Mission made a similar discovery of them. Hunting after specimens of great literature in Tamil, a language he had come to adore, Costanzo Beschi (1680–1742) lighted upon the *Tirukkural* around 1730 CE. Captivated by his discovery, Beschi set to work on a translation of the work in the classical language he knew—Latin. He thereby gave to the world beyond the Tamil world a sense of Valluvar and his legacy. His very Latin, very precise, almost cryptic, understanding of the *Kural* is what led many other societies to come to know and value the work. To give an example, the *Kural*'s cryptic opening couplet in Beschi's Latin reads like an epigram:

Literae omnes principium habent literam A
Mundus principium habet numen primordiale

Beschi's Latin translation of the *Tirukkural* unveiled the work to 'foreign eyes' as it never had been before—a defining accomplishment. His own individual perspectives and linguistic shapings did for the *Kural* what the Persian translation in 1657 CE of fifty of the Upanishads under Prince Dara Shukoh's oversight did for those epic works. Following its Persian rendering, the *Oupnekhat* was later translated into Latin, becoming the vestibule for the western world's understanding of the Sanskrit original, most notably by one of its first adherents, Schopenhauer. Beschi is to the *Kural* what Dara Shukoh is to the Upanishads. He enfranchised the Tamil text and set it afloat on the waters of world literature. Known and commented on in that hoary language by insightful scholars, the *Tirukkural* now turned from being a Tamil preserve to becoming the world's property.

BUT HE LEAVES A PART OUT

Vivifying the Book of Virtue and the Book of Wealth, Beschi, ordained priest that he was, kept Book III, the Book of Love, out of his attention. This was the translator's editorial decision. Was that all right? Perhaps it was not, for it attenuated the work's textual integrity. On the other hand, Beschi's decision to translate the work having been an individual decision he was under contract with none but his own mind's understanding with the author. And we cannot forget that Beschi's foray into a text that is sensually daring if not sexually explicit would have been problematic.

Beschi's partial translation was followed in 1848 by a French version of fragments of the *Kural* by M. Ariel, which in turn was followed in 1865 by a German translation done by the Lutheran missionary, Karl Graul. The *Kural* scholar and wildlife expert of international repute N. V. K. Ashraf points out in his most illuminating website on the *Kural*: 'Over the last three centuries, numerous scholars have taken on the task of translating the *Kural* into various languages. It has now been translated into all major languages of the world like French, Latin, Polish, Russian, Swedish, German, Japanese, Dutch, Czech, Finnish, Malayan, Burmese, Korean, Chinese, Singhalese, Italian, Urdu, Arabic and at least eight Indian languages.'

The first complete rendering of all the 1,330 couplets in English was to come in 1886, at the hands of a remarkable cleric.

A BACHELOR BRITON, ALL OF NINETEEN

When Queen Victoria was two years into her reign, a young bachelor set sail from England to the southern coast of India. The future Rev. George Uglow Pope (1820–1908) was an Englishman of Canadian descent and had been bitten deep by the India bug that led some unusual men to journey to our land and preach the gospel to 'the Indian heathen'. But this Christian missionary's fascination with India had, like Beschi's before him, another, unusual, twist to it. One might call it a sense of expectant wonder that completely outstripped his commitment to the New Testament.

Almost without exception, every missionary learnt the 'native language', if only to make the task of communicating with the locals much easier. But young Pope wanted not just to learn Tamil but to see if some jewels unknown and unimaginable to a European mind lay in it. And so, on board the ship, he began to learn Tamil with what can only be called an appetite. I do not know what book or tattered notes were available to him on that voyage, but grapple with the strange new and magnetic language, its script and its spirit, he did. So diligent was his study and so fruitful that when he landed in Sawyerpuram, near Tuticorin, in 1839, he was able to reply to a welcome address in Tamil. Pope was to stay for nearly half a century in the Tamil country, during which period he saw as many as two dozen governors of Madras come and go, and nearly twenty Governors General of India in and out of their Calcutta manor, including Lord Dalhousie. Pope, who would have heard the rumblings of the Great Revolt of 1857, the massacres in merciless numbers of British residents in upper India, and of Indians in malicious numbers afterwards, lived through those events, grew from youth to middle age and entered old age in the Tamil-speaking world doing all that he was meant to do for his Christian mission. But he also did something no one asked him to, no one expected him to and no one else could have done with anything like his elan: translate into English the formidable Tamil epics—the *Tirukkural*, the *Tiruvachakam* and the quatrains of the Naladiyar.

VALLUVAR'S VISION ENTRANCES POPE

Pope noted the elision by Beschi of the Book of Love but priest though he too was, he felt he had to translate the work in its entirety. This was his concordat with the work. He wanted to share with readers of English Valluvar's vision of the totality of life. And this not as a Christian or a representative of the 'race of rulers', but as one who had come to admire and even subscribe to Valluvar's sense of the oneness of human impulses, for good and evil, for largeness of intent and rank pettiness. He did speak of 'us', meaning, thereby, the English-speaking, English-minded, Christian presence, of course, but that 'us' was used in a sense that had nothing in it of the royal 'we'. He was in a category of observers that chance had sent to India not to scorn or scoff at it but to learn from it, albeit with eyes open to India's patent weaknesses.

BOOK I: ETHICS AND THE KURAL

The priest's calling did not leave Pope in his translation exercise; indeed, it influenced the process. Pope writes in his introduction to the work of Valluvar and his residential environ: 'Mayilapur to us is better known as S.Thomé. In this neighbourhood a Christian community has existed from the earliest times...and we are quite warranted in imagining Tiruvalluvar, the thoughtful poet, the eclectic, to whom the teaching of the Jains was as familiar as that of every Hindu sect...pacing along the sea-shore with the Christian teachers, and imbibing Christian ideas...and day by day working them into his own wonderful *Kurral*.'

He goes on to describe the *Tirukkural* as 'the one Oriental book, much of whose teaching is an echo of the Sermon on the Mount'. But more important by far is Pope's celebration of 'the thoughtful, the eclectic', in Valluvar. That—thoughtful and eclectic—is in fact the best summing-up of the *Kural*'s teaching. The work has terse statements, tightly coiled into the words. It does not have the time or space to say, 'I think...', 'Perhaps....', 'I suggest...' in quite so many words. It proposes, rather than prescribes. It leads the reader to figure out the proposition in the calm of later reflection.

What does Book I propose?

In his introduction to the translation, Pope quotes M. Ariel as saying of Valluvar and his work:

> ...its author addresses himself, without regard to castes, peoples, or beliefs, to the whole community of mankind...he formulates sovereign morality and absolute reason...in their eternal abstractedness, virtue and truth...equally perfect in the austere metaphysical contemplation of the great mysteries of the Divine Nature, as in the easy and graceful analysis of the tenderest emotions of the heart.

It would be futile and unnecessary to improve on that description.

Certain key words and phrases in that quote are worth reflecting upon: the whole community of mankind, sovereign morality, absolute reason, eternal abstractedness, virtue, truth, metaphysical, contemplation, analysis, emotions of the heart.

Reconstituting these key words of M. Ariel to summarize Book I's import, one might say the following:

Living ethically is the only way for an individual to live in society. Lived otherwise, life will spell ruin for the individual and agony for the 'family of man'. What does 'living ethically' mean? It means using the signals of the mind and the emotions of the heart to live responsibly and compassionately, in a 'humane order', as opposed to the violent jungle of moral chaos.

SO, IS THIS ABOUT THE SAME OLD THING—'BEING GOOD'?

Is the *Tirukkural* merely an iteration in the form of literary couplets of what has been said before in didactic prose or verse, testamentary texts and tracts, books sacred and holy? This critical observation is not to be contested, but it needs to be examined for its own self-refinement.

The *Tirukkural*'s message is not 'an unheard melody', true, but there is in the *Tirukkural*'s exposition an ideational increment. Where most other emphases on ethics rely on a moral, religious, or doctrinal argument for being good, Valluvar suggests that as an almost scientific postulate. I say 'almost', for Valluvar's aim is not to prove anything by means of empirical evidence. His 'code of conduct', a phrase often employed to describe Books I and II, follows the scientific method of analysis, reflection and explanation, in that he uses the procedures of sustained observation and analysis to say what he does. There is in his world view a Darwinian sense of human evolution from the chaotic primitive to the code-respecting social animal, in whom dwells an awareness of First Principles, of Creation, of a Creator, and of this thinking, feeling, invariably floundering, often regressing, frequently foolish and even perverse but essentially evolving being called Man and his inseparable companion, the hugely intelligent entity called Woman. The opening couplet cannot but lead the reader to ponder its consonance with Darwin's words:

> There is grandeur in this view of life, with its several powers, having been originally breathed by the Creator into a few forms or into one; and that, whilst this planet has gone cycling on according to the fixed law of gravity, from so simple a beginning endless forms most beautiful and most wonderful have been, and are being evolved.

For sequential enquiry and, hence, a chronological description of the phenomena under study, Valluvaresque ethics are sited in what may be called, today, the human genome and not in a scientifically and logically elusive 'conscience'.

The *Tirukkural* uses the pathways of analysis and contemplation to advance a state of balance in private living and public duty. Virtue and truth are seen in it in their pure abstraction, as distillates of experience. Valluvar's terse Tamil couplet, folded into metre and click-starting in its opening rhyme is like a Euclidean theorem—poised from the very beginning of its delineation in its brief symmetry, stable from the start in its own internal balance. It does not have to proclaim in raised decibels or flared dramatics its rather calm findings, one finding per couplet. It clinches the argument with the force of logic within the assurance of its metrical order, not to forget the strong atrium of its opening rhyme.

BOOK II: FROM BEING GOOD TO BEING POLITIC
Another departure of Tiruvalluvar from traditional moralizing is in his approach to the severely monastic concept of 'virtue', which

can become particularly intimidating in its adjective—'virtuous'. Put simply, even simplistically, Valluvar suggests through a series of his aphorismic observations that it is not just good and necessary to be good, it is pretty wise and, in modern parlance, quite smart to be good as well.

Tirukkural's Book II is where this unusual pathway to the good is laid. This Book is, very particularly, a handbook or manual for worthy dynasts, hierarchs, princes and monarchs. It is also a collection of warnings served to the utterly unworthy oaf, sluggard and licentiate who succeeds to the throne by accidents of heredity.

It is a compendium of very friendly advice from a partisan of the monarchical system to the occupier of the throne. The advice is: be wise, politic, smart, do not squander the opportunity to be a good warrior, a wise administrator, a protector of the kingdom's material and human wealth.

POLITICS THEN, POLITICS NOW, WITH LITTLE TO TELL THEM APART
Reading Book II brings vicarious comfort. Making suggestions to ministers of the king, often couched in terms of 'Don't be a fool', it shows that intrigue, slander, flattery and deceit are not new to Indian politics. Nor an itching royal palm. What is beyond comfort, and in fact, brings sheer joy, is Valluvar's assurance that when a neglectful or corrupt ruler is hated by the people his days are strictly numbered.

Tiruvalluvar knew exactly how kings, ministers, officials and councils of state fare. He has to have been someone very integral to power circles, if not a minister himself. In the delightfully timeless section that Pope translates as 'Not To Dread the Council', Valluvar urges the minister to study his briefs, be au fait with rules and then let his oratorical skills work:

> By rule, to dialectic art your mind apply
> That in the council fearless you may make an apt reply

Tiruvalluvar's advice to the ruler to take criticism from his ministers is so wise as to never be accepted. Pope translates the relevant couplet as:

What power can work his fall, who faithful ministers
Employs, that thunder out reproaches when he errs.

WARS, WARRIORS, HEROES AND THINGS THAT GO WITH THOSE

What comes as a surprise in this sage-like author with his Jainism-evoking ardour for vegetarianism and non-killing is his expertise in war. Valluvar's understanding of the mechanisms of war, warfare, battles, battlements and of combat—both hand-to-hand and between massed forces—is serious. His almost inborn sense of the use of animal power in battle is astounding. But operations apart, his sense of an army's criticality to the state is striking, as is his very specific interest—one might call it specialization—in the building, maintaining and wartime deploying of forts and fortifications.

One also carries away from the *Kural*'s occupation with the theme of war the clear sense that peninsular India in the first three or four centuries of the Common Era was the theatre of conquests and reconquests, with kings and minor feudatories resorting to battle to safeguard their kingdoms or territories or to establish ascendancy. The armies of Tiruvalluvar's south had infantry, cavalry and elephant regiments. They also had, if Book III's side references to the loved one being at sea 'in action' is an indication, maritime forces under them. The weapons described are still those that were used before the advent of gunpowder. It is a commonplace belief that the north was subject to invasions and war and that the south was spared that travail with the result that its culture and cuisine, architecture, literature and the arts in general, are stabler than those up country. This is a very 'broad-brush' view. Romila Thapar says in Volume 1 of *A History of India* (1966) in the chapter titled 'Conflict in the Southern Kingdoms *c.* AD 500–900':

> The political history of the Deccan and further south evolved...
> from the conflict of two geographical regions, the western
> Deccan and Tamil-nad—the vast plateau areas enclosed by
> mountains along the coasts on the one hand, and the fertile
> plain south of Madras on the other.

War is war and a soldier killed in a battle between neighbouring kings fighting for domination is no less dead than one killed at the hands of an invading army. The trauma for civilians is the same in both. Just as Tiruvalluvar talks of god but names no deities, he talks of wars but describes no specific armed engagements, no borders or territories, no dynasties.

The *Tirukkural* has not been read, or read sufficiently enough as social history, for the reason that it is undated. But I do believe that just as some murals, such as those at the Brihadeesvara temple in Tanjore have more than one layer, each 'film' speaking of a different concern, a different age, so also do Valluvar's couplets bear layered messages, the one-shot ones on the surface and others beneath the formal aphorism which give, unintentionally almost, vignettes of his times, their mores. These need to be excavated with fine analytical instruments and then dusted carefully, sometimes with a single-hair brush, to reveal the inner cuts in relief.

Had Valluvar cited episodes, named kings and dynasties, the gain to historiography would have been instant and immeasurable. We would then have dated Tiruvalluvar with reasonable accuracy and used his comments to interpret historical passages. But there would have been a loss as well, and a serious one at that. The abstraction of the discourse which is a Valluvar signature and a Valluvar strength would have been lost to the dubious particularisms of dates and names, the passing trivia of changing contexts. As they are, the 1,330 couplets give us wisdoms from the vats of experience, leaving us to conjecture the hinterland of those wisdoms.

And yet some historical facets emerging from the *Kural* are not to be ignored. Only an in-depth paper on the social history contained in the *Kural* will be able to do full justice to that vast theme. But a sketch of that dimension of the work may be attempted here.

The *Tirukkural*'s world knows an intricate polity, complete with a monarch, an assembly, ministers and counsellors. It also has systems of financial control, police and security forces, and espionage agencies. It has, of course, as we have seen, an army and something like a navy. Romila Thapar's description of life in the peninsula in the chapter of her book cited earlier includes the following which could well portray scenes from somewhat earlier times, portrayed in the *Kural*:

1. For three hundred years after the mid-sixth century three major kingdoms were involved in conflict. These were the Chalukyas of Badami, the Pallavas of Kanchipuram, the Pandyas of Madurai.
2. Much of the revenues went to maintain an army...the king preferring a standing army under his control. The army consisted in the main of foot-soldiers and cavalry with a small body of elephants.
3. ...the Pallavas'...navy had other purposes as well as fighting. It assisted in the maritime trade with south-east Asia...
4. Assemblies were of many varieties and at many levels, including those of merchant guilds, craftsmen and artisans.

Valluvar's Tamil country has disparities, with men of wealth and those who are destitute. It knows splendour and squalor, literacy and ignorance. It knows disease and a fairly standardized system of medicine and medicament, with apothecaries and the ancient equivalents of nursing orderlies.

It has a place, and an institutionalized one at that, for the arts. It has the forbear of the modern sabha. Valluvar writes of halls where dance performances take place before assembled audiences. As it has courts, so it has courtesans.

Ascetics and mendicants were around, one may say, in good numbers. Valluvar suggests that some of them were truly elevated, some fraudulent—a familiar story!

Handicrafts are vital to society and to the economy. Metals, including gold, are known. Working on metals is advanced. Jewellery is made and worn extensively.

Agriculture is well developed, as is irrigation. The criticality of rain is understood not just in a vague sense but in fine detail.

Valluvar has a climatologist's deep insight into the making and unmaking of clouds, of rain cycles and the impact of rain on the land and, even more strikingly, on the sea. I have earlier referred to the foreshadowing in Valluvar of Darwinian insights. Valluvar's understanding of what rain and its failure does—not just to crops but also to human relations—finds a parallel in Darwin's words:

The action of climate seems at first sight to be quite independent of the struggle for existence; but in so far as climate chiefly acts in reducing food, it bring(s) on the most severe struggle between the individuals, whether of the same or of distinct species, which subsist on the same kind of food.

But the same scientific Valluvar can also occasionally give us scientifically unacceptable cameos, such as this one in Verse 55:

God aside, before her husband she genuflects
And the rain! It rains in buckets

The family is an established and cherished institution, with marriage holding an important place in it. But the woman is subordinate to the man, especially the married woman to her husband. That person, the householding man, is something of a demigod to be worshipped by his wife. Social prejudices abound. The transgender, for instance, is clearly not on par with men and women. Superstition is rife in Valluvar's world and Valluvar himself is persuaded by 'signs', 'omens' and 'traditional belief'.

But then a man can only be that much ahead of his times.

NATURE THEMES IN VALLUVAR

Sangam literature—a term that scholars like Kamil Zvelebil question, preferring the word classical—is enriched by a classification of emotions and situations that are either agam (inner) or puram (outer) and are also associated with a specific physical landscape. Agam landscapes, generically called tinai, include kurinji (mountainous regions); mullai (forests); marudam (agricultural land); neithal (coastal regions); and paalai (deserts).

The *Tirukkural* has a vivid landscape of its own with the sky and the sea, mountains and arid land, farms and forests, rivers and rivulets forming a visual backdrop to the human theatre that unfolds. Wildlife and forest life are not out there in the life Valluvar paints but up close. His sense of different species of bird life, animal life and plant life is by any standards, absolute or relative to his times, remarkable. Moving from the worm to the elephant, the seed to the palmyra; avian, mammalian, amphibian, reptilian, marine and botanical subjects dot the *Kural*. As do, of course, what we would call climatological themes. Only deep deserts, ice and snow elude his vision, for sheer lack of personal acquaintance, which in itself is an admirable self-regulatory principle.

Elephants feature regularly in the *Kural*. The tiger makes its appearance, but not the lion—a significant detail from the natural history point of view. Among trees, the palmyra is prominent and the coconut totally absent—a botanically interesting nuance. The flowers mentioned do not include the rose. Water bodies in the shape of rivers, lakes and village ponds are cited to illustrate human moments, predicaments.

What makes Valluvar's observation of nature unusual is his ability to metaphorize what he sees into human situations. A couple of examples illustrate this skill of his:

Verse 527

The crow crows when it lights on food and caws, 'Come, kin, and join!'

Good and only good will come if we sit with kith to dine

Verse 481

Sunlight-dazed, the owl yields to the crow
Star-crossed, the king falls to his foe
Or if I were to put it straight
And not bury truth under words' dead weight
It's when you're weak or distracted and don't know what to do
That men who want to hit you will come out and get you
So get your action right
And find the fitting time to fight

Valluvar's close observation of wildlife behaviour is brilliantly reflected in the following couplet, about what may happen to a crocodile.

Verse 495

In waters deep and dark the crocodile murders at will
But outside his water-fort he's himself an easy kill

If the *Tirukkural*'s three Books were taken as its progeny, Book I would be The Thinker. Book II, The Doer. Book III, its one and only but very truant daughter—lovelorn, woebegone and very, very full of herself—would be The Lover.

Book I is an education, Book II an instruction, Book III a delight—to read, to visualize and be puzzled by.

In terms of its content, Book III is a standalone. How a tract that is frankly about love in its personalized aspect of physical longing and that, too, expressed in terms of female longing, should form part of a work on individual and collective ethics, is puzzling. But in terms of style and the calibre of its Venba metre it is neither different from nor lacking when compared to the first two Books. Had Books I and II not existed, and Book III alone been extant as the work of Tiruvalluvar or any other poet, it would have attracted due notice and appreciation. It would have been regarded as a dramatized *Kama Sutra* with a longing for unceasing physical contact and sexual union being discussed in a sequence of cameos.

It is no surprise then that, good Jesuit that he was, Costanzo Beschi left it out of his translation. No surprise either that Rev. G. U. Pope writes with disarming candour about 'Kamattu-pal', as the Book of Love is titled in Tamil: 'Kaman is the Hindu Cupid. Hindu ideas differ from our own. This prejudice kept me from reading the third part of the *Kural* for some years...'

So, for 'some years', the book's defining translator did not even read this part of the book in an act of self-censorship. Prevalent rumours about its 'degeneracy' must have influenced the padre. Book III *is* sensual and the reader who wishes to read more sense into its verses than the author intends, should find no difficulty in doing so. There are couplets which lend themselves to an interpretation that crosses the line of what, in company, could be called decency. But there is such a thing as the general latency of any piece of writing—Book III is sensual without being carnal, physical without becoming a class in progenitive biology. It lifts the veils of privacy but does not let the drapes of propriety fall.

It is captivating in parts. And it has an undeniable dramatic appeal which, I am surprised, has not become a string of padams or javalis choreographed in the style of Mylapore Gowri or with the elan of Tanjore Balasaraswati. Tiruvalluvar describes a hall where dance was staged to a full and appreciative audience. Clearly, a form that could have been Bharatanatyam's precursor was strong and vibrant at the time and we can assume that the romantic was not absent from it. The 'She' in Book III could well have been the subject and the presenter of such a form of dance. Seeing a soulful rendering of Dharmapuri Subbaraya Iyer's javali by Shijith Nambiar and Parvathy Menon in *Sakhi Prana*, a short film directed by Rajiv Menon, I could imagine Tiruvalluvar's 'She' as a padam's protagonist. Many vignettes in Book III evoke Kshetrayya's padam, *Paiyada Paimeda,* in which the dancer uses the telltale Tamil 'ayyaiyo' at a moment when no other exclamation can express her emotion. The 'ayyaiyo' was 'refined' by puritan presenters in later decades into 'ammamma', a form of Sanskritization, as explained by Carnatic vocalist T. M. Krishna (who renders the padam with 'ayyaiyo' and not 'ammamma'). Book III leaves its protagonist's archetypal 'ayyaiyo' with its distinct sensual coefficients unabashed.

Book III is not without flaws. It is a string of independent cameos and therefore seems disjointed and does not arrive at some clear stand on love, its loss and its regaining. This flotation of intent and accomplishment seems to be out of joint with the terse exactitude and unfailingly assured tenor of Books I and II. Valluvar does not amble in Books I and II. He does not, in Book III either, but there is in the gait, pace and stride a rhythm that seems different from those of Books I and II. Beyond the charming and even delightful description of a lovesick woman's dalliance with her seafaring lord, no larger purpose is served by Book III. It can be of value to the study of obsessive compulsive neuroses, in this case of a lovesick woman for a male idol.

And yet, I cannot say that Book III is the work of another hand. Apart from the fact that the use of the Venba metre in it remains exact and that Book III has been part of the earliest extant templates of the *Kural,* there is one more aspect of Book III which points to the author being none other than Valluvar. And that is in the treatment of 'public opinion', of what others say, what the village thinks. In this echoing of a background chorus, Book III shares much with recitals of a public voice, a social commentary, a civil conscience that adjudges individual action in the earlier Books.

VALLUVAR ON WOMEN

Tiruvalluvar is passionate about man, the householder and woman, the homemaker. Gender equality is not a concept that detains Valluvar. Indeed, parity or equality between man and woman is outside his imagining except in what Periyar E. V. Ramasami calls 'the state of love and desire'.

The *Tirukkural* has been written by an extraordinarily enlightened man for men who, the author thinks, should be helped to be enlightened. There is an assumption that the woman is meant to be by man's side as a happy and uncomplaining performer of household duties, an upholder of gentle domesticities, a proud bearer of progeny and tradition. She is man's ornament. Should she wish to play a role beyond that, we are cautioned, she can be an embarrassment—if not an actual risk—to her husband's standing and to the family. She must have the wit to be able to fulfil her man. And he must have the foresight to fasten the latch on conjugality. But she too must do something; she must use her own vigilance to further secure the latch by a 'lock'—her own intuition—to protect her chastity.

Valluvar despises unethical men; he loathes the henpecked man and the cuckold. Marriage is held up as a creed and 'touching another's wife' a crime. Though female sexuality is discussed with candour in Book III, the woman 'who sells her body' comes in for harsh, ringing criticism.

The *Tirukkural*'s view of the woman has come in for lively analysis at the hands of none other than the social reformer and thought-changer, Periyar E. V. Ramasami. He yields to no one in his admiration for Valluvar's genius but is critical of the *Tirukkural*'s handling of the position of women in society. In a series of essays published in *Kudi Arasu* titled 'Pen Yen Adimaiyaanaal?' (Why did the woman become man's subordinate?) are included two pieces on the *Tirukkural*'s delineation of women. Written between 1928 and 1932, when controversy over Katherine Mayo's *Mother India* was raging and the Sarda Act was being enacted to raise the age of consent, it is a remarkable body of progressive thought. Some of the chapters of Periyar's book presage Bertrand Russell's radical *Marriage and Morals*. Saying, 'I am...a bit confused with the stand of our Tiruvalluvar', Periyar observes 'I feel extreme slavishness and inferiority has been introduced in the context of women in the 6th chapter (Virtue of a Life-Partner), in the 91st chapter (Being Led by Women) and in a few individual couplets'. Displaying remarkable insight into the concepts of 'chastity' and 'husband-worship', Periyar says that, in the normal course of the way our society looks at things, a woman is supposed to regard her husband as lord and master, and that Tiruvalluvar does not depart from this view. In another powerful essay in the same newspaper he cites legends about the devotion of Valluvar's wife, Vasuki as she is believed to have been called, towards her husband to exemplify this image of husband-worship.

VALLUVAR THE MAN

Known not by his name but by the title given to him—Tiruvalluvar—he has been accepted, in G. U. Pope's words, as 'undoubtedly one of the great geniuses of the world'. He is described by Pope as having been, by avocation, a weaver and by today's community categorizations, a Dalit. Some Brahmins have claimed he was one of them, Sri Vallabha! Fame opens doors, it does.

Tradition reinforced by the evidence of date-identified Tamil works situates him in Mylapore, Madras, now Chennai. But no one knows quite when he lived, or exactly where. Any time, it is hazarded, between a hundred years before Christ or seven hundred years after. That makes him a likely contemporary of Kalidasa.

No stone tells us, nor any ancient leaf, whether he was a sage or minister, teacher, soldier or even king. There is a school of thought that maintains he was a king in the tracts around the present Kanyakumari. He could have been any or all of those, for, he writes on all those human types as one of them. Whether he was a king or not, he knew what poverty meant. He knew that very well. So well, in fact, as to literally curse the Creator for having created poverty. 'That men should have to beg, may He like them, wander accurst', he writes.

Some have held he was Jaina. If he was, he has very consciously kept that affiliation quiet. We may not disturb it.

He had compassion for all life, not in some mindless way but in a very modern, very humane way. Cruelty was abhorrent to him not because some god or saint had called it evil but because his brain, his heart, the very tendons of his being, told him it was ugly, wrong. In this he anticipates William Blake's *Songs of Innocence* which has 'Each outcry of the hunted hare. / A fibre from the brain does tear.'

What we can discern, by the evidence of his couplets, is that he lived somewhere along the Tamil coast. We can feel in his couplets that describe the sea what Sarojini Naidu in her poem 'The Coromandel Fishers' calls 'the kiss of the spray and the dance of the wild foam's glee'. He knew his sea for sure and the pains of the earth along it. He knew the land, its tiller and the twists of his mind, his fate. Like a meteorologist, he scanned the sky for the raincloud. Like a mineralogist he knew the value of what the earth held in its deepest clasps.

He knew animals, birds and plants well. Well enough, one might say, to be called in today's terms, a 'nature-type'. And he knew not a little about the human body, its ailments, and how to treat them. As we have seen, legend has it he was happily married. Perhaps he was. But he knew the thing called love. Who can be sure if that love was entirely home-bound? Perhaps it was.

All we know, and know for sure, is that he wrote what he wrote— small, tight aphoristic verses, in metred, measured might. He was a grammarian of grammarians. Because he knew the chains of versification, link by link, he could break the manacles of thought. His couplets, called 'Tamil epigrams' read like Time's telegrams. Telegrams speak in the words, signal in the gaps. Telegrams convey tidings both good and sad.

So do Valluvar's.

And they are always urgent.

A BOOK FOR ALL TIME

Although we will never know with any certainty which century the *Tirukkural* was written in, no work has suffered less by being dateless and nameless. In times of ethical lurchings, whether among leaders or led, among nations and institutions, Valluvar's masterpiece is a beacon of plain common sense and high wisdom.

In their compressed layering, the 1,330 kurals are like a diamond mine. They arouse uncommon interest and sparkle in varying facets at each reading. They are thereby, in the immediacy of the messages they convey, so timeless and timely that they strike the reader in each generation as something that has been said for them today. And which is also the reason, as N. V. K Ashraf points out, why without the backing of any denominational group, any religion or sect, they have remained so compelling.

The non-sectarian voice speaking to humanity as a whole makes it a book for all people everywhere and for all time. It is in its universality that the book is and shall always be a book for the future.

A book for the future is, by that very description, a book which levitates ever so slightly above the present. It remains a tad too ideal, just that much too precious, too *fine*, to be of the here and now. Despite that timeless element to its tenets, what makes it more, much more than simply a classical manifesto or collection of tenets is the fact that much of what it says remains applicable and relevant to this age, the ages that have preceded this one, and the ages to come. It is, quite simply, a book for all time.

Book I

BEING GOOD

Chapter 1

THE CREATOR

1

As 'A' is of every alphabet the primordial letter
So is god the world's very fount and progenitor

2

Your learning's idle, incomplete
If you haven't placed it at that source's feet

3

Long lives the one who embraces the feet
Of him who graces the Holy Flower's seat

4

Those who see he's from craving free
Can walk on earth as free as he

5

Who in god's praise builds his life
Protects his home from care and strife

6

Those who follow him who has conquered the senses five
Live a long and good life and its trials survive

7

None may the mind's great torments meet
Save in the refuge of his redemptive feet

8

You cannot at redemption's shore arrive
Unless to attain his grace you strive

9

Who stands unawed by the versatility of god
I'd call, I'm sorry, a mindless clod

10

If you'd cross the sea of birth and death
Seek at god's feet his grace's wealth

Chapter 2

RAIN

11

Joins sky to earth, it does, life on our planet to sustain
And so 'heaven's true nectar' is how we call the rain

12

If food is what keeps us alive
'Tis rain that gives food its life

13

Our sea-bound land to thirst is doomed, and to hunger and pain
When clouds turn hard and their rain-trove enchain

14

When rainclouds go back on what seemed like their word
Ploughmen turn still, sullen their oxen herd

15

When it stays off, the rain ruins through and through
Only to return, smiling, to its victims' rescue

16

If the skies don't let their pearl-seeds flow
The grass in its seedbeds won't grow

17

The ocean's teeming wealth cannot but decay
If from its thirsts rain stays away

18

When the heavens turn parched and dry
Temples too must neglected lie

19

All charity ends, all penance, atonement
When by drought the skies are rent

20

Even as Nature, without water, goes pitifully a-begging
Man's compass without rain loses its bearing

Chapter 3

ASCETICS

21
Renunciates' lives must—on this all books agree—
Reflect the rules which their codes decree
22
To enumerate the virtues of the venerated great
Would be as tough as counting the late
23
This world allures, the other world draws
The true ascetic in this follows the other world's laws
24
Strength comes from fencing in the senses five
And nursing a seedbed for the next life
25
Of the sense-curbers' self-restraining finesse
Indra, lord of the firmament himself, is witness
26
The great attempt things that are hard to accomplish
Lesser beings from such situations vanish!
27
He can rule the world who knows the ways well
Of the senses five—taste, sight, touch, sound and smell
28
The weight of a nation's thought is known
When by the written word its worth is shown
29
At the height of his powers a sage may be afire
But the lofty moment over, his rage must retire
30
They alone can the title of 'Knowing Ones' use
Who with book wisdom humane care fuse

Chapter 4

VIRTUE

31

Virtue confers honour and makes prosperity swell
In the virtuous life alone does fortune dwell

32

Nothing, but nothing serves life better than virtue
And nothing mars it like its forfeiture

33

Virtue is a house with many rooms to try
Find out how good 'good' is and why

34

That mind's called 'virtuous' which is unstained
When 'tis not, what matters what it is named?

35

When envy, rage, lust and foul speech, these four
Don't deflect you, you're on virtue's path secure

36

Befriend virtue right now, not 'sometime later'
At your dying hour it'll rush in to help; it's no procrastinator

37

Some the swinging litter bear, some swing in the litter
Some deeds give you the high seat, some the journey bitter

38

Good deeds done each day grow into a mighty rock
Which all winds of harm will resolutely block

39

True joy in virtue lies
Nothing else can raise you in your or others' eyes

40

What ought to be done is on virtue built
What ought not, on guilt

Chapter 5
DOMESTIC LIFE

41

The good householder, at Order Two, on home duties bent
Frees Orders One, Three and Four, for higher callings meant

42

To the recluse, the parlous and even to the dead
The householder stands in trusty good stead

43

The householder's duties these five, in right measure, hold
The spirits of the dead, god, guests, kin, with himself enrolled

44

He who earns to spare and eats so to share
Protects his progeny's line from ill-fare

45

No grace exceeds, no value lies above
Within a family the bond of love

46

When home and home life can with virtue thrive
What other good need one seek or for success strive?

47

He whose hours at home are lived with natural ease
Heads all those who live on nobility's high crease

48

The householder helping family and friends
Is no less ascetic than who to his own salvation bends

49

A good householder's life's for all of us to see
And, if we're half wise to—what's the word—'copy'

50

Who house-holding duties with virtuous care performs
Meets heaven's prescribed norms

Chapter 6
THE HOMEMAKER

51
In the careful use of her husband's means
She is her home's queen of queens

52
She a hundred gifts may have, but if at minding the home is slack
Its happiness will, quite simply, crack

53
No want be-grimes the housewife tended home
No shaft of light enters the wife-disdained dome

54
No greater strength for a householder can there be
Than his wife's steadfast loyalty

55
God aside, before her husband she genuflects
And the rain! It pours then in buckets

56
She who keeps herself and home from all harm
Comes to be known as a haven of calm

57
Vain is the watchful eye, vain the padlocked door
If a woman's sense of self-respect is not its guarantor

58
When to her groom she stays true
Heaven's glory becomes her due

59
If the wife is what a wife's not meant to be
The husband cannot be a lion in company

60
'A blessing' is how grateful husbands call their wives
Wives, in turn, give them children to prize

Chapter 7

PROGENY

61

The gift of children to learning and good deeds inclined
Is un-equalled by others of any kind

62

Those who children rear
The mesh of rebirth will spare

63

Children are man's great good fortune
With their good deeds is prosperity hewn

64

Ambrosia's a poor drink, as I've heard
Before the slop a child's finger's stirred

65

To a parent the child's touch is the joy of joys
Its little voice music, all other sounds—noise

66

The flute can please, the harp appeal to those and only those
Who haven't heard their infant's lisp in which the sweetest music
flows

67

No gift can match, no boon excel the giving by sire to son
Of that learning which makes him with the learned, one

68

Pleasing it is to hear oneself called wise
More so to see an offspring's wisdom cause surprise

69

More than when she bore her son, the mother feels fulfilled
When she hears his learning called 'gold's very gild'

70

He makes his father proud to whom men say 'Well done,
Blessed is the man to have you for a son'

Chapter 8

LOVE AND THE LOVELESS

71

No ban can send love hiding, no law its spirit confine
One shy tear will excavate its darkest, deepest mine

72

The loveless, wholly self-absorbed, in themselves stay mired
The loving, in their very bones, by care for others, are fired

73

If the soul is clothed in flesh that feels both soft and rough
It is to get a sense of what it means to love

74

Love leads to the union, no less, of two mental worlds
A union in which one into the other's world furls

75

The life lived in love is a gainer full twice over
On earth in joy and then in heaven's clover

76

Evil abounds; so love has to be tough
In a world that's so, oh so very rough

77

The merciless sun scorches the writhing worm
The loveless heart shrivels in its arid home

78

Joy in a loveless life is as much of an impossibility
As flowers on a sapless tree

79

The human frame will be an empty shell
If the soul within is lonely and unwell

80

Life is life when lover and loved both live it together
Loveless men are but—what shall I say—bones clad in leather

Chapter 9

THE UNWELCOMING

81

Good housekeeping also means keeping open doors
For guests to walk in, be cared for, by you and yours

82

Be it food 'fit for the gods' or a meal of lesser fame
To gorge alone, guests unfed, is an utter, damned shame

83

Old wisdom says, 'Who the guest with welcome greets'—
And believe me, it's got it right—'with bounteous plenty meets'

84

As also, 'When he to every gentle guest courteous care extends
Her blessing to him in a myriad ways Fortune gladly sends'

85

'Grain'll ripen unsown on your field if your guest you welcome
make
And only after he's eaten, of what remains, partake'

86

'Who welcomes the coming, and waits for the future guest
Has safe for him, in heaven's warm parlour, a long-awaited rest'

87

Don't count too soon the fruit of your vague 'kindnesses'
They are the worth, exact, of your guest-care pluses and minuses

88

'My life goes waste,' you cry in pain and yet you cry in vain
Remember, when need knocked on your door you too showed
disdain

89

Misers spurn house-guests their wretched wealth to hoard
Their empty hearth their fate laments as does their lonesome
board

90

Touched by greedy fingers, a flower's fragrance will fly
Untouched by care, a guest's expectant heart must die

Chapter 10

RIGHT SPEECH

91

Men of the light are men who care
Their words humane, hard messages bear

92

Greater gift than the gift itself is the gifter's gifting style
Winning more than what is given is the giver's giving smile

93

The gift of kindness, not gifts in kind, help the one in need
The first is given, the second flung, to feelings paying no heed

94

From ill fates' brutal swipe is the kind-worded girded
And gets a grateful world's thanks ever so lovingly worded

95

Modest, gentle speech a human being adorns
The rest, cheap tinsel, are vanity's loans

96

To the seeker of good the words come right
Virtue seeks him like darkness does light

97

Words that uphold virtue and the codes of right and wrong
Raise the moral tenor and make its timbre strong

98

Words that are kind, tender and not vexed
Spread joy within your world and in the next

99

Knowing kind words heal hurts in the soul
Why speak words that will bore in it a hole?

100

When words abound that soothe, why use those that swipe
With ripe berries around, why pick those unripe?

Chapter 11
GRATITUDE

101
A good turn done is a heaven-born gift you cherish
Ask 'Will he repay it?' and it'll perish

102
A helpful act howsoever slight
When timely, acquires true height

103
To help without thinking 'What's in it for me?'
Is to be, for the helped one, vaster than the sea

104
Help, like the millet seed, may itself be small
But its spirit stands like a palmyra tree, tall

105
Don't judge help by its shape or size—'is it large or is it small?'
See how it has met a need, if it has met it at all

106
When with ill-fortune you feel mighty sore
Just recall the pure ones who helped you in your woe

107
You will in all your seven lives bless
Those who've helped you in your distress

108
If you've been helped, don't forget it, not for a single day
But if you've been wronged, you must forget it—and right away!

109
When the wrong done to you hurts like a sore
Recall one good the wrong-doer may've done and forget the woe

110
Forget to do good and you may find salvation yet
But forget gratitude and you're headed for destruction's net

Chapter 12

IMPARTIALITY

111
When justice's scales their balance maintain
We can be sure we are in equity's reign
112
Honest wealth bequeathed endures
And heirs from grief inures
113
Thinking 'Oh who'll ever know?' do not to temptation bow
Wealth's stealth will out one day; so quit that thought right now
114
Who lived right and who lived wrong
Progeny'll disclose in the burden of their song
115
Tides high and tides low drench us, turn and eddy
In this big bog the upright man stays high, dry and steady
116
If with wrongdoing you're minded to dally
Know: ill fortune's already in your alley
117
The world salutes an upright man
No matter how small his estate's span
118
To be judged 'upright' and win men's trust
You have to be, like the balance, just
119
If the heart not be twisted or tangled up in knots
One's words will come clear from clear thoughts
120
The trader true is the trader who minds his clients' stake
Held in level balance with his just profit's take

Chapter 13

SELF-CONTROL

121

An inner flame of rectitude links us to Heavenly Light
The damp cold wick of baseness to Endless Night

122

Self-control is wealth, guard it with zeal
No other strength can match that steel

123

It's smart, not just good, to practise self-control
And thereby gain true contentment, as deep as it is whole

124

If from self-control you don't slip or swerve
Your worth'll rise mountain high on life's every curve

125

Modest bearing befits life's every single station
But in one who's rich it is a distinction!

126

If your fortune is through the seven worlds to spread
Draw in your five senses as the tortoise does its head

127

Of the many slips on the slope of life's slippery slips
The worst is the careless word that passes through our lips

128

The hurting word to the hurting man some instant joy may bring
But be sure it will return to sting the stinger's sting

129

The blistering welt of a fiery rod may, in time, congeal
But the withering lash of a scathing tongue will never ever heal

130

Who rising anger quells by the power of self-control
In composure dwells and lets that virtue save his troubled soul

Chapter 14

THE WELL-REGULATED LIFE

131

A life without discipline is shaky, insecure
Guard your conduct and your well-being ensure

132

Learning, watching, inculcating, do all that and more
But turn to your own discipline to secure your door

133

No one's 'born noble' on this earth
Conduct makes you trustworthy, not birth

134

A forgetful scholar may regain on books his old grasp
But misconduct will forever sever his stature's ancient clasp

135

Gripped by envy no man can move ahead
He'll collapse under that load of lead

136

As sure as a life of honour leads to fame
One degraded must end in shame

137

Regulate your life and earn deserved credit
Unregulated, fall—even when you aren't the culprit

138

The well-regulated life is a well-sowed seed
The ill-regulated one, a pain-giving weed

139

The well-regulated possess a mindfulness
That'll speak no base thing in 'forgetfulness'

140

They learn in vain who don't remember social dues to pay
The bookworm's life's a waste though it bores through tomes its
way

Chapter 15

NOT COVETING ANOTHER'S WIFE

141

He who knows the codes, what's what and who's who
Won't be a fool another's wife to woo

142

Of all the fools fool enough to join the ranks of fools
None beats the fool of fools who for the next-door woman drools

143

You'd be better off a corpse, I'd say, cold dead
Than lust after her who to your care's been entrusted

144

The great can look great fools if led
By foolishness another's wife to bed

145

'Trifling', you might call the affair, 'a mere harmless game'
But the hidden trampoline will open you to shame

146

Hate, sin, fear and disgrace dog his life
Who violates another's wife

147

Husband, father, friends and all such dew-like ties
Will then, like steam over a melting pot, vaporize

148

Adultery is no part of manliness!
Propriety is, virtue is

149

He is thought 'good' who rounds this earth of seas
Without as much as touching a woman who's not his

150

If in other trespasses he's shown himself a naif
In keeping off adultery he has acted wise, acted safe

Chapter 16
FORBEARANCE

151
The man who hurts and digs her up the earth does not disown
So must we, the wrongs done to us, with forbearance condone

152
Forgiving the wrongdoer, in life's book, has grace
But forgetting the wrong itself has an even higher place

153
The unfed guest walks out cursing the miserly host
The unwanted friend comes right back, like wave to patient coast

154
If you must see your prestige grow
Your forbearance levels must never be low

155
Revenge beats a tinsel drum, heard and then dismissed
Forbearance hews a golden rock, by compassion kissed

156
Vengeance beguiles the fleeting day
Forbearance has everlasting sway

157
When hurtful ill is caused to you, give that ill a shock
Pity the ill-giver's 'illness', reverse ill-will's clock!

158
A haughty pride it is that makes men cause you harm
Know that, and by forbearing calm, all those men disarm

159
If a householder keeps his cool on hearing choice abuse
He's no less of an ascetic than the 'saint' who makes the news

160
Men of the world who forgive insults and worse
Are greater than hermits who, in hungry caves, scowl and curse

Chapter 17

NOT ENVYING

161

Discipline's code gives a clean pride of place
To the virtue called un-envying grace

162

No greater misery can there be, no load so huge and heavy
As the evil weight that bears all down called—you know it—envy

163

The folly of follies is watching another's joy or gain
And, comparing it with one's own, feel self-pitying pain

164

Be wise, keep envy at bay
Only fools go that fetid way

165

If you're jealous, you're scripting your own ill-fate
You stand as your own enemy, stone in hand, at your own gate

166

If you eye what others have with envy's burning eyes
Misery and penury will strike those you prize

167

Fortune and Misfortune are sisters who work together
Fortune dislikes envy and directs it to her sister

168

The 'good' aren't, just because they're good, from ill-luck immune
Envy will with hellfire bring you ill-fortune

169

'Why?' the thoughtful wonder, 'why on earth is't so
That the blameless suffer ills and the wicked unpunished go?'

170

Happiness the envious will never earn
Nor the un-envious ever lose but Envy just won't learn!

Chapter 18
NOT COVETING

171

Coveting what belongs elsewhere's wrong and worse
For it brings upon your home a just resentment's curse

172

What's by right another's, don't try to go and get
Just don't, what's another's, ever covet

173

Of no value are the baubles of entertainment
For those seeking a deeper contentment

174

Whose senses have been honed to restraint
Know by covetousness only misery's gained

175

Wasted are book-wisdom's large realms
If greed your judgement overwhelms

176

'None can breach,' the householder can claim 'my iron-clad moral door'
But ruinous greed can poison his life's very core

177

The fruit of a tree from stolen seed can never ever taste sweet
Your tongue just mustn't crave what is not yours to eat

178

If you watch with envy another's rising tide
Be sure Fate will take you down her slippery slide

179

Who stays away from Greed and Greed's daughter, Folly,
Will in want be helped by Fortune most prodigally

180

Who lusts after another's goods lusts himself to death
He stays safe who eyes no one else's wealth

Chapter 19

ILL-TALK

181

His words might reek of sulphur, his deeds appear dim
But if his neighbour he hasn't defamed, some good he has in him

182

Better far the rascal whose speech is laced with bile
Than the back-slanderer who greets you with a pasted-on smile

183

Better be dead than blacken a friend from afar
And on his close approach turn into honey that tar

184

Standing face to face, your open punches aim
But don't send hidden darts—that's an act of shame

185

Virtue's about the heart not tongue, and goodness about grace
Words can no more play the deed than a mask can fool the face

186

Don't spread stories about your neighbour others to regale
Your neighbour can with equal ease, your own tales retail

187

Words can slice the heart, split open the brain
They can make friends vanish and leave you in lonely pain

188

Will those who with gusto their friends' faults relate
To concoct non-existent faults ever hesitate?

189

The earth bears with charity the load of vicious abuse
That men heap on absent men in talk that's called 'loose'

190

If only we would stop the practice of finding fault
Fault-free our world would become by that one single halt!

Chapter 20

THE WORTHLESS WORD

191
Words must be spoken to some purpose
Tattle's more offensive than the tattler may suppose

192
Speaking worthless words to the wise
Is like—in fact, worse than—harming friends you prize

193
Who speaks without purpose, measure or sense
Declares to the world his mind's incompetence

194
Neither the learned nor the rabble
Have use for babble

195
Men of so-called rank are also great at babbling
But bunk being bunk their bunk too shares their ranking

196
High among the masters of faff
Are men whose words are chaff

197
Better far to stay unheard
Than speak a single worthless word

198
The wise use their words with care
They don't float them idly in the air

199
Those of vision will from speech refrain
Than speak thoughtlessly or in vain

200
Speak, if you must, words that bear good fruit
Not words that patience rob, and time loot

Chapter 21

DREAD OF EVIL DEEDS

201

The sinful, sinning away, see no 'sin' in sin
The wise, shunning it, see sin as hellfire's terrestrial djinn

202

Sin from sin spreads and grows
How exactly it does that, only fire knows

203

Evil cannot evil quench
Nor stench out-stench stench
Wisdom it is to not hate your hater
To not want to torment your tormentor

204

Plot not even half-seriously another's ill or harm
There's a higher justice that such plotting will disarm

205

Evil acts will not make you rich
They poverty with misery stitch

206

If low-minded men treat you to some low-minded act
By very different behaviour their lowness counteract

207

A way out can be found from every corner called 'blind'
But not from the pact with evil you've signed

208

Like your shadow dogs you from behind or before
Nemesis follows any evil done, of this you can be sure

209

Watch out for dangers from the evil you have done
You're very likely to be by yourself undone

210

He who evil spurns
From all ill his freedom earns

Chapter 22

OF A BEFITTING HELPFULNESS

211

Duty is its own seed and fruit, its own labour and wages
The rain no gift expects beyond freedom from clouds' cages

212

The honest rich commit their riches for others' good
Not to shameless self-indulgence as the vulgar rich would

213

Neither up in high heaven nor here on earth's lows
Does anything equal helping those who are our fellows

214

He who helps others breathes, feels and is alive
He who does not does not know the meaning of 'life'

215

Fortune fills the good man's cellar with grain
Like the village pond swells up with rain

216

A large-hearted man coming into wealth
Is like the village fruit tree bursting into health

217

A tree from its tissues healing substances provides
The generous man his wealth's goodness to others guides

218

The duty-minded even if themselves in need
Won't pause from paying others heed

219

The large-hearted poor man has but one worry: lack of means
To help him or her who on his lean shoulders leans

220

If ruining yourself to stop another's ruin is what's
demanded of you
Ruin yourself, again and again, to your helpful
purpose stay true

Chapter 23

GIVING

221

What's given to the needy is given from one's giving purse
What's 'given' otherwise is commerce

222

Giving with respect to meet another's need
And without ego, beats hollow the joys of receiving
Don't give just so heaven counts that deed
Giving's no giving when done to receive heavenly blessing

223

'What can I give? I have nothing!' is low-souled and mopey
Sharing whatever little one has is true philanthropy

224

The deep-lined face asking for alms displeases
But giving the copper in your purse
And seeing a smile wipe away that face's harsh creases
Will open, in a while, a new universe

225

One's sunken abs are carved by fasting's toothed fangs
But a greater joy, by far, is ridding another's hunger pangs

226

Relieving hunger in another gives the pleasure
One gets by securing a rare trove of treasure

227

Who delights in sharing with the hungry his plate
Hunger will never intimidate

228

Crazy are they who stint on help to the needy
Only to die leaving unused their mint—so, so greedy!

229

Wretched is he who must for his food go begging
But wretched more who behind closed doors sits pigging

230

Who wouldn't, if he can help it, dodge death's bitter call
Who, if he can't help others, could bear to live at all

Chapter 24

RENOWN

231

More than as 'a generous man' no better renown
Can a human head crown

232

On this all agree: when the needy ask
To give is in deserved praise to bask

233

Recognition, praise, renown—these in the world stand high
Without those three backing your life you'd have lived to but die!

234

Deeds of virtue performed on earth the gods higher rate
Than those of sages who in high heaven levitate

235

This only the wise know: to lose wealth or not to gain
Doing what feels right within
Is to not lose, rather, to win
To die, likewise, is not to cease to be but to live again

236

If walk you must on the public stage, be sure you suit your part
If not, it's time for you from there to depart!

237

'Let people think what they think'
Is the surest way in sin to sink

238

Virtue bringing esteem, some say, is like human birth
If your deeds no fame generate, what is your life's worth?

239

Innocent crops will shrivel and die
If the earth's run by men disgrace can buy

240

The blameless live their lives un-blamed
The fameless leave life's wick un-flamed

Chapter 25

COMPASSION

241

To be kind, to care and perhaps to love is to have true wealth
Even the vile have the other kind that rhymes so well with 'stealth'

242

Teaching eminent sense, all creeds at heart 'compassion' teach
That's what their teaching's really about—peoples' hearts to reach

243

Charity glows and glowing keeps all within aglow
As grimness grims the grim world we know

244

Love embraces the loved ones, holds them heart and soul
It also cleanses the loving one and leaves him feeling whole

245

The breeze-kissed earth knows life is about grace
And keeps those safe who a life of grace embrace

246

Who all goodness forsake, all kindness and all grace
Are the miserable ones who then the very opposite face

247

This world, heartless, the unworldly breaks
The next world, sublime, the worldly unworldly makes

248

Worldly 'stuff' un-stuffed can be re-stuffed again
But those who lose love can never love's realm regain

249

Who his mind won't use must a moron be
Who his heart won't, is cold and stony

250

When a tormentor torments you with torments you can't bear
Recall the time when you were the bully that you were

Chapter 26

MEAT

251

How can one not see the ugliness of eating meat?
How can one made of flesh another's flesh eat?

252

He who does not bolt his home its loot cannot prevent
He who does not halt meat-eating can claim no refinement

253

The butcher with his knife cuts up living, breathing things
The glutton with his teeth completes the grim proceedings

254

Don't hide behind the butcher's blade saying, 'He kills, I only eat'
You're the one that whets the knife that makes the thing called
meat

255

What is heaven if not the grace of peaceable living?
What is hell if not the guilt of ravenous animal-killing?

256

If you give up your meat-craving and your life thereby 'upgrade'
Why will anyone in his senses practise this gory trade?

257

What is meat but the wounded flesh of that which was once alive?
Think before the once-throbbing morsel you next try to hive

258

If you wish, as you should, that your soul be liberated
Think: this once lived, breathed, moved, till it was beheaded

259

The thousand offerings of this and that to reach some mythical
merit
Are bilge! Just stop killing things to eat them—that's when you'll
reach it

260

Just picture this: all living creatures in thankful gladness throng
Clasping hands, in praise of non-killing man, they sing a happy
song

Chapter 27

PENANCE

261
Penance is about feeling another's pain as one's own
And for any pain caused, quietly to atone
262
To offer true penance you must know how to atone
Else, be honest, stay as you are and leave penance alone
263
If ash-smeared and long of beard you're able to be all pious
'Tis only because some reg'lar folk work as your want-suppliers
264
'Tis said penance empowers the penitent to punish or protect
So penance is done to kill foes, and friends from doom resurrect
265
'Tis thought penance works, works for sure, right here and now
So men do penance to get what they want just any old how
266
They fulfil themselves whose penance is not vainglory
But 'penitents' who stay world-mired tell another story
267
Gold glows as the furnace burns the coal
The ascetic shines as penance mines his soul
268
Now he's 'something else' whose mind has mastered his limbs
And who, quite rightly, the world a master deems
269
That true penance powers the ascetic is not at all in doubt
By making him oblivious to life, it even puts death to rout
270
If the world teems with distress the reason's quite clear
Of penance's de-stressing power the world doesn't want to hear

Chapter 28

INAPPROPRIATE CONDUCT

271

Your hypocrisy makes your five senses laugh
Your guile can't fool them, not by half!

272

Men of high repute shrink to midget size
When their stricken conscience meets their guilty eyes

273

A man's holy robes can hide his sinning mind
A tiger skin can help a cow free pasture find

274

The man clad in a sage's guise sinning in secret vies
With the fowler hiding behind a bush his prey to surprise

275

If looking very law-abiding you really are anything but
Know the law'll soon find you out and you'll then be in a rut

276

Saying 'I've quit it all' but staying in thought quite profligate
Will not shield the wily eyes of the fraud renunciate

277

Shining and ruddy like a kunri seed he looks
But look closer! From the sage's secret inside a black 'nose' snooks

278

Many there are, many too many, who in holy waters dip
When inside their skins hides a moral drip

279

Don't go by looks: the arrow, smooth, clean, pierces
The harp, bent, makes music; don't go by appearances

280

The gleaming pate and flowing beard in saints that we applaud
Are fraudulent if their conduct with our codes doesn't accord

Chapter 29

NO FRAUD

281
If heaven's joys you seriously want, give up thoughts of Fraud
Cousin to Cheating, Deceit and Guile, Fraud even puns on God

282
For what's not yours don't crave
Have some sense, behave!

283
Stolen goods may come to you tip-toeing
But they'll just vanish—flying out on a very fleet wing

284
Greed for fraud's vile pickings is a sickness
That brings with it a pain which is endless

285
'Goodness' means zilch to him and 'grace', 'compassion' nix
Whose ever-clever eyes and feather-light fingers wait to work their
tricks

286
Foolish not to be wise it is, wise not to be foolish
Fools drool over thoughts of fraud which the cautious wisely
banish

287
The cautious wise, watching their steps, to a higher state advance
The cunning wiles of fraud they shun and their mental poise
enhance

288
The mind of measured wisdoms is to virtue host
The mind of cunning wiles is cleverness' boast

289
Soaking in vice's deep soak the soaker soaks deep
And so soaking soaks into his un-waking sleep

290
The fraudulent's fraud buries him in his own fraud's sod
Staying off fraud, the un-defrauding fraud defraud

Chapter 30

VERACITY

291

Truth is that which isn't a lie but is more than 'not untrue'
Truth is that which has no ill that can hurt you or you or you

292

A 'lie' may lie and be the lie that liars lie about and yet it could
Be classed with truth if it blesses someone with good

293

The heart, the heart, it knows the true from the false
It burns, yes, burns when falsehood breeds within its walls

294

The soul, the soul, it glows when truth dwells in it
It lives, it lives in the souls of all truth-lit

295

Great is penance, greater still when it comes with charity
But greater far is truth in all its purity

296

No greater fame there is as on truth's shoulders rests
Without the load of penance it passes e'en tougher tests

297

It matters not, it matters not if other good deeds happen not
As long as truth happens to be your life's first and last resort

298

Water cleans your outer frame, truth the soul within
No sin there is that sin remains if truth has made it kin

299

No lamp lights a light so bright or ever can
As the truth within lights up the dark life of man

300

Match it with this good deed here or that virtue and merit there
Simple truthfulness is, quite simply, without compare

Chapter 31

NOT BEING ANGRY

301

Getting mad at someone weak or under your charge—is just not
done
And anger matters little if you aren't boss and will ne'er be one

302

It's mad to be mad when being mad's futile
But to be mad when madness hurts is worse—it's downright vile

303

Wrath wreaks wrath on the wrathful
Be wise, shun wrath and, for your own good, stay cool

304

Of all ills and tempers ill temper's the very worst
In the dark art of killing joy it stands a hated 'First'

305

Anger's quick as quick can be so you've got to be quicker
Else, it'll knock you flat with 'There, that's for those who bicker'

306

Wrath burns that which is close and that which lies afar
It can set the precious family raft blazingly afire

307

Anger hurts the angered one more than him who made him sore
The fool who smites the ground smites his hand the more

308

The many tongues of anger's fire burn as the furies burn
So sense demands that you from anger turn

309

Hold back that rage, hold it right back, for then you gain not lose
The tide on which your life's raft must cruise

310

Those that wrath burns up are as good as dead
Who burn up their wrath are sages, no less, 'tis said

Chapter 32
EVIL

311
Wealth raked in by harming others, like any wealth, can wow
But know you this: such ill wealth the codes do not allow

312
The malicious are plain rotten, only ten times worse
So bear no malice, please, if you're not to be a-curst

313
Do not harbour vengeance not even against a knave
Retaliation will make of you malice's faithful slave

314
Make the evil-doer see his evil's shaming face
By doing him one perfect act of grace

315
The eye that's glued to learning is blind to the scripts of pain
The ego just steamrolls the heart in the service of the brain

316
Have you ever felt pain as in 'felt' and in 'pain'?
Yes? Then you'll never give it to another, not one dram or grain!

317
To not give, to never ever give to another, woe
Is the highest virtue you can gain or temptation forgo

318
Who has felt his heart scooped out, his soul rendered dry
Could he, would he, causing another woe, even try?

319
Life loves to mime and so if you do evil in daytime
By night-time, be sure, evil will hit you, rhyme for rhyming rhyme

320
The very evil he's done will over the evil-doer spread
Its brooding wings in wait till it can strike him dead

Chapter 33

NOT KILLING

321

'Kill not,' enjoins Virtue. Could it, would it, do anything else?
It wouldn't, for Virtue is Heaven's ally, just as Killing is Hell's

322

Share your meal with the hungry, protect those threatened by
death
This is what Goodness enjoins—non-killing through life's length
and breadth

323

In being good, not killing comes first
With not lying coming next

324

'What's the true way' you want to know, right?
That which does not the cult of killing incite

325

A 'Yea' to the great who life and its laughter renounce
But 'Hurray!' to those who go further and slaughter denounce

326

Life-thirsty death will from its hold release
Those who say 'No-killing, please!'

327

Give up your life for another's to save—any day!
But take another's life? No way!

328

Profit is gained from any trade as of course it must
But profit gained from slaughter can only disgust

329

Killing for trade tops the pile
Of jobs that are by nature vile

330

Feeling pain you wonder why you're having to bear it
Perhaps a slaughter in your past it is you're now to requite

Chapter 34

IMPERMANENCE

331

That life's tree will always be in leaf
Is a foolish and fond belief

332

They fill the hall in eagerness the great dance to see
No sooner is it done, they exit with rapidity
Wealth's the same—it swells as the hall's seating sells
And shrivels as the concert crowd melts

333

Knowing all wealth goes fast
Use it to make something that'll last

334

The day, I see, as a day, of course, but also another way
As a fine-toothed saw that saws life down day by day by day

335

Before your tongue goes slack and that rattle rocks your throat
Don't fail to do what you must to deny death's sway its boast!

336

Here today, gone tomorrow
Fun today, tomorrow sorrow
'Wondrous' indeed is this odd world
(For want of a better or odder word)

337

None can tell if she or he will last the day today
And yet we go, fools that we are, planning and plotting away

338

As the restive bird, singing, abandons its nest
So the soul flees the body, tired of being its guest

339

'Death's but a nap' says old wisdom
But birth? A break in the soul's freedom

340

The soul is a wanderer, a wanderer is she
She sits in the body, just waiting to flee

Chapter 35
RENUNCIATION

341
The more from yourself you yourself untie
The faster from the pain of that tie you fly
342
There is in giving up a joy of its own
Give up, give up now, to taste that joy unknown
343
The senses five must each in their place retire
If renunciation is that to which you aspire
344
Keep the thing and you won't be able to give up on it
Shed it, shed it fast, if you want its hold to quit
345
This heavy solid mould of clay, this thing which won't let go of life
Is the biggest hurdle, can you not see, to freedom from life's strife
346
The 'I', the 'I' and 'my' and 'mine' are a weightless weight
That shed fast will take you through freedom's gate
347
Who hold on to holding's hold, hold on to life's old woes
That 'holding' holds you in its grip and relief withholds
348
There's this thing called the net, life's constricting net
Renounce it and free yourself or don't and be throttled by it
349
And there is this thing called attachment, to things small and big
Give that up if you want to be free from life's constraining rig
350
There is this hold, though, the hold that holds all, the holder and
the held
To that hold fast, hold long and well, and in its rapture melt

Chapter 36

TRUE KNOWLEDGE

351

Born of and into error, by taking false as real
Our present and our future we seal

352

Banish the dark, view the light by seeing false as false
And from all delusion freed, hark to the mystic vision's calls

353

Freed from all delusion you'll feel heaven near
And the sod you stand upon distant though right here

354

Trifling are the five-fold senses' refrain
Unless on them an inner light you train

355

If you don't see what's behind that which you see
You're as blind as blind can be

356

If to see the real and to know its truth you learn
You're on the path to the place from which there's no return

357

If your mind knows what's of heaven and what's of earth
It need not ponder any more upon birth, death and rebirth

358

When folly causing births and all life's ills departs
Knowledge of higher calling starts

359

When you cling to the true clinging, which clings not to this earth
You will be from sorrow freed and from all that comes from birth

360

When lust, wrath and delusion no more strangle you
From all pain you'll be, believe me, through

Chapter 37

GIVING UP DESIRE

361

The seed of seeds, say the wise, is the thing called desire
From which flow the twins, birth and death, in a ceaseless gyre

362

If it's desire that you desire it'll clasp and burn you in its fire
And then you'll have to burn desire to flee its incinerating pyre

363

Abjuring now what the senses crave is advice, or call it 'tip'
For a future happiness where you'll a different nectar sip

364

'Break loose from desire' it is wisely said, 'and purity regain'
By doing that you will a sense of the true attain

365

Giving up is no giving up if desire's not given up
And without giving desire up 'renouncing' is just a cover-up

366

Very cunning is desire
In its consequences dire

367

He who works with respect for the work
Not driven by desire, will do well—be he king, be he clerk

368

Affliction is not known where desire is not seen
Where desire is king, sorrow follows as a hapless queen

369

If desire has been put out, misery is in rout
And even life on earth is heaven—or just about

370

Drive out desire from your life's lodgings
And end, at once, sorrow's many-sided jinx

Chapter 38
FATE

371

Effort that brings wealth and indolence that gives grief
Are both the gifts of fate that permits no relief

372

The rich going bankrupt, the dull turning bright
Happen very exactly under fate's oversight

373

There's what's called book learning, then there's the thing called
wisdom
The first's about life's broken parts, the second its glorious sum

374

Fate's made those two: the wealthy and the wise
The two stay two, stay two they do, separate, with no ties

375

The good can be grief-stricken while the wicked prosper
None can change fate, the silent account-keeper

376

You'll never keep what's not yours even if you bury it deep
You won't lose what's rightly yours, left open as you sleep

377

Fate has for each laid down a share of wealth that's fair
But to want beyond that a greater share is wrong—beware!

378

What can the wretch in utter want renounce—his own want?
Past deeds have thrown him to misfortune's bitter taunt

379

When in luck men thank that luck and their lucky stars
When not in luck they blame their fate and life's one big farce

380

No power can match, no skill defeat fate's undisputed will
Try as he might, contriving man will stay fate's puppet still

Book II

BEING POLITIC

Chapter 39

THE GREATNESS OF A KING

381

These six—troops, happy subjects, wealth, aides, friends, trusty
guards—

Make a king king and master of the kingly arts

382

And these four—gutsy, giving, sage and spright

A king must be for his kingship to come right

383

Awake he must be, in eye awake, in brain informed and bold

If on his kingdom the king's to have a hold

384

That king is king who respects virtue, and vice repels

Is courage itself and in foe-harrying excels

385

For the king's attention to his kingdom's wealth to fruit

He must guard its source and its produce even-handedly distribute

386

When easy to reach and of pleasing speech, of that king

His subjects praises sing

387

When his words soothe and his arms protect

The multitude he rules, that king is said to have 'a kingly effect'

388

The 'god on earth' title is justly his

And his alone who rules with a sense of justice

389

That king shields his realm who does not shield his ears

From bitter words of warning and of counsel has no fears

390

Help, grace, poise, devotion

Are a mighty king's definition

Chapter 40
LEARNING

391
Learner, learn your learning full well and fault free
And then make your learning with life's living truths agree

392
Numbers and the alphabet amount to human eyes
Life's mysteries to decipher, its facts to recognize

393
When eyes are used for learning eyes may be called eyes
When not, they're mere blockhead sores in eyes' disguise

394
You greet it with an embrace, part from it with a hug
Learning's the good friend you meet and leave with a tug

395
The scholar begs for knowledge
The beggar for his food
To the first we give the stage
To the second a coin crude

396
In soils of sand, the more you delve the more rush its springs
So too in learning, the deeper you go the more bounty it brings

397
The scholar each land befriends, each town makes its own
The unschooled dies at home a nomad, lonesome and unknown

398
Learning's a store, a treasure scholars acquire
It has all and more than what the seven worlds aspire

399
Learning gives the learners joy, it gives them that and more
It gives them love of learning and the wisdom at its core

400
Wealth can crack, shrink, even vanish
Learning does not tear or ever tarnish

Chapter 41
IGNORANCE

401
With the learned to seek converse but not for that honour prepare
Is to move draught pieces about without the chequered square
402
The unlearned toss flimsy words around and at their sounds exult
Like those un-grown who know not love yet want so much to flirt
403
Some blockheads are very smart: they won't open their traps
And just by that 'I know' look, pick up fond backslaps
404
But most blockheads unblock their tongues and bray with fluency
Declaring to the world around, their minds' vacancy
405
A blockhead's head is plain foam and tongue a piece of flab
When all in council are speaking sense the blockhead will just
blab
406
Those who learning resist
Like a barren field just exist
407
Those the mind's ray of light, sharp-pointed, does not guide
Are puppets in bibs and baubs, to ignorance's strings tied
408
The wise man with no wealth, his poverty can shake
But the rich man without learning will one day just break
409
Those 'low born' but learned are no longer 'low'
Those born 'high' if unschooled are just lumps of dough
410
The unlearned is to the learned what the beast is to man
So, learn, man, learn from the learned whatever you can

Chapter 42

LISTENING

411

Through your ears to hear, to listen and to understand
Is to make gold of grain and golden grain of sand

412

Only when what's to be got from listening has been got
May one turn to what from eating may be brought

413

Offerings turn stone to gods
Listening makes humans of gastropods

414

Learn by listening if from reading you cannot
That'll be the staff from which your grip on life is got

415

If you hold a staff in hand, slippery grounds can hold no dread
With learning held in a virtuous hand, well-being lies ahead

416

By hearing the good let good come to the good
And give to the good what only the good to the good would

417

No slip of slipping tongue slips through the slipping lips
Of those who've heard lessons on how to keep off life's slips

418

It is one thing to hear, quite another to internalize
One's about not being deaf, the other, being wise

419

Only if you hear what's worth hearing
Will you speak what's worth speaking

420

Ears can hear—and taste—sound
The tongue to but one sense is bound

Chapter 43

POSSESSING KNOWLEDGE

421

Wisdom's a fort, O king, of strong wall and will
To awe all foes from its commanding hill

422

Wisdom's a goad to bring your mind back from all loiters
To the path which prudence reconnoitres

423

Wisdom's the sieve that keeps the grain
And lets the rest just drain

424

Wisdom listens to others' thoughts and from them draws
Lessons to blend with its own to make its subtle laws

425

Wisdom's the flower that opened once is open for all
Not favouring the dawn or closing up at nightfall

426

As the world lives so live you and to its mores incline
It is wise, always, with the seasons to combine

427

Wisdom's a compass that guides you to the road you need to take
Not stumbling between dry well and pond to miss the brimming
lake

428

Wisdom's the instinct which says, 'Fear that which harms'
Its opposite is that which sneers, 'What's fear?' and caution
disarms

429

Wisdom's the forethought that helps you to prepare
For that which you cannot stop but can perhaps repair

430

Wisdom's the blessing that makes what's rich rich
Unwisdom's the curse that unstitches the stitch

Chapter 44

FAULT CORRECTION

431
Pride, rage and the pettiness come from base desire
Shun those three and you have hope against misfortune's ire

432
If the king is a stingy fatpurse or grinning bag of bluff
He commands no more respect than a stuffed sack of fluff

433
'Fault?' you may protest, 'this millet-sized foible's no fault!'
But the foible's a future palm whose crooked growth none can halt

434
If from fault you're free you own a very special kind of wealth
And if not, well, you have a fatal kind of ill-health

435
Felicity's a funny thing; open, yet shy
Guard it from evil as you would golden straw from fire

436
That king is king who'll first his own faults own
And only then those of others bemoan

437
Put off what should be done and you put your wealth at risk
Do it betimes and be sure its increase will be brisk

438
Of all the faults in humanity's list
The worst is what men call avarice

439
Few natures can be sicker than the one called 'smug'
Don't be called a self-complacent 'ugh'

440
Hug what you love but don't ever flaunt your love
For your foes will then get the hugged, the hugger they will shove

SEEKING THE AID OF GREAT ONES

441
For friends the king the virtuous and the wise must choose
And with due care or else be prepared for boos
442
The rounded wisdom of the well-weathered great
Helps remove present travails, wards off perils that wait
443
Adopt the great high-souled as your own, your very own
For a king as king and as man, is truly, truly, alone
444
Those in this small world who want to approximate
Greatness cannot do better than live beside the great
445
Wise counsellors are for a king his very eyes
In choosing those he must go by wise advice
446
The king who allied with the great dwells
Need fear no knavish knells
447
That king will rule well and long
Whose ministers can upbraid him when he does wrong
448
The king whom no one checks, no minister corrects
Does not have to wait for foes, himself he vivisects
449
'No principal, no interest' is trade's well-known law
Not heeding wise ministers is a king's fatal flaw
450
Ten times worse, yes, ten times, than incurring the hate of foes
Is it to leave worthy friends and friendless face life's woes

Chapter 46
WRONG COMPANY

451
The great will the mean avoid
The mean from the great will hide

452
Water turns as sour, saline or sick as the soil it goes through is
And so we become what our friends are—froth or foam, fuzz or
fizz

453
More esteem is got by the company you keep
Than by the lunge of your words or by your mind's leap

454
Wisdom's not the mind's find
It is from friendships mined

455
Thought and deed, clichéd indeed, can work like a pair of twins
Nurtured in pure company, that pair laurels wins

456
The band of the pure can give us a line of virtuous folk
That no ill can threaten nor ill-deeds ever revoke

457
Does 'being good' one's wealth raise?
They say it does but it does more—it makes us merit praise

458
The right kind of mind works to one's great good
But wrong company can rot that good like wood

459
The noble-hearted the next life's happiness will inherit
Because good companions have paved the road to it

460
Good companions, we know, are a great help in life
But bad company, take it from me, is impossible to survive!

Chapter 47

ACTING AFTER DUE CONSIDERATION

461

Kings don't just jump into things—what the venture'll cost, what
it'll bring

What its future value'll be: these are things on which they think

462

Kings must, first, consult trusty counsellors, then on their counsel
reflect

And only thereafter act; that's what's called being circumspect

463

If 'gain ahead!' means loss of present cash

King, pause! That undertaking's rash

464

From a venture of which the nature's unclear

Stay away, if you opprobrium fear

465

Don't blunder, king, into an act that can cause offence

Such bravado gives the foe a field with a good fence

466

To do the unbecoming is to open the door to ruin

And to not do what you should be doing is a hole to sit and rue in

467

To plan well is to plan a win, not with chance to amble

That plan's no plan which wants with luck to gamble

468

You may have an army of great size

But if your plan's no good

You'll come to rue your enterprise

And your hopes will be—dead wood

469

There are in men these things called tendencies

Good works can fail if these the king knows not nor sees

470

The world sees a king's great 'ends' but sees his means as well

It deems the ends good only if the means ring a clean bell

Chapter 48

POWER

471

Weigh, king, weigh well, before setting out to fight
Your strength, that of your friends
And grasp well your foe's might
In order that your war, king, in your triumph ends

472

The mind is all—by which is meant, quite simply, all
It must know what is to be got and how
In that 'what' and 'how', king, stay you firm and tall
A king must know how to hold his realm in awe

473

Many a king has rushed, blind and blundering
To a war he was not ready for and fallen
Dazed and downed by his own folly, wondering
Why his ego was so stupidly swollen

474

To the joys of concord a stranger, a glutton for applause
Such a lonely and languid king will walk into ruin's jaws

475

Overload is overload be it of rock or feather
Peacock plumes in bulk can a wagon's axle sunder

476

A tree's top is its very tip, its skyward journey's end
The 'climber' must stop at that top or to his end be sent

477

Giving has its measure due, its scope and its limit
Stay within that for your wealth is not infinite

478

No matter if the earnings are meagre; no calamity'll beset the
realm
Just see that the spendings the earnings don't overwhelm

479

There's this thing called the proper scale—hold it straight and level
If you are not to lose by recklessness what you have as you revel

Or if I were to put it more blunt
(And not for polite words hunt)
If you don't stop boiling the stew
You'll end up mopping the goo
480
Charity's charitable art needs charity done to its own heart
When at home your own bowl's hungry, don't throw a feast in the mart

Chapter 49

KNOWING THE FITTING TIME

481
Sunlight-dazed, the owl yields to the crow
Star-crossed, the king falls to his foe
Or if I were to put it straight
And not put truth under words' load of weight
It's when you're weak or distracted and don't know what to do
That men who want to hit you will come out and get you
So get your action right
And find the fitting time to fight
482
You must align life's grain strictly to your times' refrain
And thereby tie to a sturdy rope present and future gain
483
If your means are right there's nothing beyond endeavour
Except, of course, that vital thing—the right propitious hour
484
The world will be yours by right
If you act when the hour's right and right your action's site
485
If a king bent on conquest bides his time in calm
Chooses his moment and then strikes, victory's in his palm
486
The battering ram steps back, recharges, and then lunges
So does the strong man hold back his rage before he plunges

Fire burns the one it seeks and the one who holds the torch
So the wise let the flame of their anger subside then with the
smoulders scorch

488

Courtesy's not an idle grace but a weapon of another hue
It can make the foe bend his head right down before you

489

Opportunity's is a rare knock heard few times and far
Know it, seize it and reach your goal by its surprising power

490

The heron stands still, wings furled, waiting for its prey
So like the heron does, with one snap, your prize waylay

Chapter 50

KNOWING THE PLACE

491

Ringing the enemy is vital, closing his routes of escape
If, knowing his guts, you do that you've caught him by his nape

492

Combat skill is vital and courage, man to man
But nothing can replace the fort as a battle's high command

493

An army's size matters, yes, but is by no means all
What matters is vantage, hideouts that lie deep and lookouts that
stand tall

494

The foe's best wrought plans will fail if you stand strong
On better ground and with clarity of aim go for him headlong

495

In waters deep and dark the crocodile murders at will
But outside his own water-fort he's himself an easy kill

496

The vessel matters but only where it can head on
The chariot's useless on water, the boat on land is carrion

497

Might matters as do guts but what matters most
Is the right plan to use on mountain, forest, coast
498

Size matters but strictly relative to space
Deploy your size by the site, case by each case
499

And there's this: your foe may be no more than foam
But stronger than you he is if fighting from his home
500

A tusker of fearless eye and matchless foot if trapped in a slough
A cunning jackal will spot and in its canine jaws devour

Chapter 51

CHOOSING THE EXECUTIVE

501

Test the person to see which of these four
Your trust, wealth, pleasure and life, he values more
And if you find he values the first, you can rest
Your man's been found after the best ever test
502

Born to light where no disgrace can touch nor dishonour shame
Yet to repute attentive—these are the codes of the hall of fame
Don't choose one unafraid of sin
A king's court needs gold, not tin
503

No one is perfectly learned, no one perfectly wise
A lack here, a fault there need come as no surprise
Select a man of good intention
Don't look endlessly for perfection
504

Humans being imperfect 'tis best to put them to test
And see them as they are, not what they protest
See where he's strong, where weak
And a fair balance seek

The best test is the test that tests all claims to goodness best
By matching claim to deed, deed to claim and scorning all the rest
506
Trust the householder, not one with no house to hold
The kinless hug every licence with matching lies being told
Don't choose the uncommitted
A king cannot be by floaters cheated
507
Being guided by the heart in matters of trust
Is, in a court, not just unwise but worse than the worst
To one in love
A crow can look like a dove
508
Don't trust the untried with your trust
A king should know his caucus
509
Hold trust back till you are sure you have trusted right
After that hold nothing back from your trusted knight
510
Once entrusted hold nothing back
Distrusting the entrusted of insecurity will smack

Chapter 52

SELECTION AND EMPLOYMENT

511
He who weighs right and wrong and stays with the right
Is the one the king must trust, else be troubled by hindsight
512
Rely on him whose mind on raising revenue dwells
And under whose sharp eye odds abate and prosperity swells
513
Loyal, sharp-minded, clear of thought and from avarice free
That man is fit to be your trustee

Tested, trusted, found to be with all the right virtues replete
Some may yet be unable some tasks to complete

The king's reliance should fall not on a favourite
But on the resourceful one who at work shows merit

516

Will he perform the allotted task and within the right hour
Are questions a king must ask the man before giving him power

517

Satisfied that the man and his given task cohere
The king should leave it to his care

518

Each has a skill to which mind and hands bend with ease
Once spotted, that skill should become his field of expertise

519

Hard-working men have their ways which at times are loud
A king who frowns on informality is not by luck endowed

520

The king must check each day if works go right and well
And if they do his kingdom's fortunes cannot but swell

Chapter 53

CHERISHING ONE'S KIND

521

In times lean and mean kin show what kinship means
By timely help they reveal the true meaning of genes

522

Surrounded by helpful kin is to be in an arbour of flowers
Which, unfading, make fragrant life's testing hours

523

A life not embraced by a family's bond
Is like an unprotected and waterless pond

524

Surrounded by caring kin your wealth will increase
Taller with each ring of love, stronger within every series

525

Him who loves to gift his kin with love
They hold to be all worldly things above

526

Gifting love and restraining wrath are twins that go together
To make the wise man truly liked in every clime and weather

527

The crow crows when it lights on food and caws, 'Come, kin, and
join!'
Good and only good will come if we sit with kith to dine

528

The king sees all equally yet gives with differentiation
This to one, that to the other, after careful consideration

529

When some kin, hurt, go away, find out the cause therefor
They will return, then, glad of heart and gone will be the sore

530

When some who left, unprovoked, on their own, return
Let them in but confirmation to a rigorous test adjourn

Chapter 54

UNFORGETFULNESS

531

Wrath numbs intelligence, giddy joy even more
It makes you so forget yourself as to wrath outscore

532

When wealth forgets a man, his wisdom withers away
When man forgets his calling, his strength loses its sway

533

The unvigilant of mind carry no conviction
This precept is found in every disquisition

534

Be he within a fort's stout walls, a coward stays a coward
Be he rich and mighty, the forgetful is deemed a laggard

Too lazy to foresee it, he cannot forestall the mishap
Unvigilant, he tumbles to doom's waiting lap

536

Mindful be at all times, in all places and situations
And you will be the wiser for those ruminations

537

Mindfulness is victorious in all deeds, tough or not
When the mind is awake no act goes waste, no task is ever forgot

538

The mindful man who seizes that which is meritorious
Journeys through his seven lives victorious

539

When intoxicated by the joys of your prosperous state
Think of those whose lives by mindlessness were laid waste

540

Each aim and every goal can be reached without a doubt
If the light in the mind that says, 'Do it!' never goes out

Chapter 55

JUST RULE

541

If your enquiries and conclusions are unvaryingly just
Your reign will be called good as it must

542

All creatures look up to the sky for rain
All subjects to justice in the king's domain

543

If the priest's word carries weight and men for honour vie
It is because ahead of them a king holds his sceptre high

544

The king who loves his subjects is by his subjects loved
And at his feet gather the trusting and beloved

545

Where the king wields his sceptre well with laws and codes in train
There the rain stays to cycles true and gilds the fields with grain

The lance rules the battlefield but the sceptre's that which wins
A kingdom's fame for might and right are two inseparable twins

547

The king guards his realm, yes, but who guards the king?
His sense of doing right by each and every thing

548

The king who isn't easy to reach is blinded by his biases
His nemesis is certain, whatever its shape and size is

549

To guard his subjects from foreign foes and from those who break
the law
With severity is a king's bounden duty, his mandate, not a flaw!

550

A king's order of death the criminal to immobilize
Is akin to saving the shoot of grain a weed to throttle tries

Chapter 56

THE CRUEL SCEPTRE

551

The murdering sinner sins
Less than misgoverning kings

552

The robber's lance-wielding arms demand: 'Hand over!'
The king's sceptre-bearing greedy palms whisper: 'Hand under'

553

The king who doesn't scan the day for wrongs done in his realm
Nor spends it being just has misfortune his kingdom overwhelm

554

A king whose sceptre on justice and mind on counsel does not rely
Will see his wealth elope and his prestige fly

555

A tyrannical king's wealth simply wears away
Under the acid tears of subjects in his sway

556

Doing right brings to the king a great flaming fame
Not doing right extinguishes that flame

557

When heavenly rain stays off, the earth in silence dries
When kingly grace holds back, life in the realm in agony dies

558

When the king becomes a greedy boor
It is worse to be rich than poor

559

As the king goes off course and makes illegal gain
The skies turn off and rob his realm of rain

560

When the king lowers his guard, cattle lower their yield
And sacred texts, lying unread, no influence wield

Chapter 57

PENALTIES

561

He is king, a king is he, who trails crime's dark beat
Then so punishes the criminal that he'll never such crime repeat

562

He is king, a king is he, assured of a heavenly glow
Who makes the guilty feel for sure
The weight of the falling blow
But hidden in that blow the light of justice even more

563

But the unworthy king is assured of infamy
Whose subjects live in dread of his tyranny

564

Once the cry 'Our king's a tyrant' is out
His days get numbered, his reign nears rout

565

The king who's hardly ever seen and when seen looks oh so grim
Should know his royal days are as few as his image is dim

The king who in speech is harsh, and cruel in the way he sees
Should know his joy of kingship, undeserved by him, flees

567

Words that grate and penalties that far exceed the crime
Are the rough file that flays the days off the king's remaining time

568

The idling king who leaves hard work for other souls to do
And then criticizes them will his idleness rue

569

Foes will capture one day and mercilessly slay
The king who builds no fort to keep them at bay

570

The tyrant king consults fools and fools himself thereby
The earth, helpless, watches this, wan, worn and wry

Chapter 58

BENIGNITY

571

If the world can smile and laugh and thank kindness for being
there
It is because in the monarch's breast there stirs a goodness rare

572

The world gets its happiness from simple folk of worth
The worthless are, of course, a dead weight on earth

573

Musical instruments misjoined to the song jar
So can harsh eyes, at first meeting, that precious moment mar

574

For the eyes to make an expression ignite
They must glow with an inner light

575

Compassionate, kind eyes are eyes
Else they're sores that traumatize

576
Eyes fixed in sockets with no ray of care
Are like trees fixed on earth with no fruit to bear
577
Those who don't sorrow internalize
Cannot be said to have seeing eyes
578
Those who know what 'benign' means and give to it their all
Can feel the world belongs to them and never feel poor or small
579
Those who know what 'benign' means scorn or belittle none
Even men on punishment row with compassion are thereby won
580
Even when he sees a host his drink with poison infuse
The benign won't—for etiquette's sake—the toxic glass refuse

Chapter 59

DETECTIVES

581
On his suite of spies and on books on spies
Let the king depend as he would on his own eyes
582
What goes on in his realm, who does what and why
These the king must learn each day from some reliable spy
583
Spies who bring not weighty news, but foamy froth and fluff
Waste the king's time and weaken him with all that blubber and
bluff
584
The spy must watch the king's foes, of course, but also his officers
and kin
For in threats to the monarch's power those can be to foes akin
585
Designing guise and disguise are in spies an expertise
As they hunt their secret prize unsurprised by prying eyes

Beards, beads and begging bowls make holy men of spies
And hide their narrow-slitted eyes in that four-B disguise
587

Spies must get the whole truth out—inside outside upside down
And then report the whole of it—verb noun and pronoun
588

Spies are spies not supermen and can go wrong or worse
So kings must see through his spies' purple prose and verse
589

The king must see to it that no spy knows another
And go by the sum of what three spies say—unknown to the other
590

The king must not on spies outward marks of faith confer
For spies are meant to work strictly under cover

Chapter 60

ENERGY

591

The wealth that counts is not the wealth that mounts
But the energy which life's hurdles surmounts
592

The wealth that counts is in the mind, in its soul's energy
The wealth outside, facile and fleet, is mere dramaturgy
593

'Have lost my wealth, have lost my all,' the man of will cries not
Possessed of the higher wealth he knows what he has got
594

Fortune seeks and finds its man of will
For it values him who ever works and never idles still
595

Just as the lotus rises with the lake and then blossoms in the
bower
The man of will rises with his will's own power

If your aim is to rise and rise ever higher
That thought is in itself a 'rise' against challenges dire

597

Even as a shower of arrows cannot make an elephant shake
Nightmares cannot make a man of strong will quake

598

The man without will can never hope to attain
The strength needed to deal with diverse men

599

The great elephant with his sharp tusks thrusting out
Will yet, with the tiger, wisely avoid a bout

600

A mind of will aspiring ever higher is the mind that will excel
Lesser minds like dry trees are fit only for fuel

Chapter 61

INDUSTRIOUSNESS

601

A family's pride and honour will sputter and die like a lamp
If sluggards let its good old wick go cold and wet with damp

602

With indolence around no fruit of effort can thrive
Banish indolence if your household is to survive

603

The sluggard lets his sluggish ways imperil all
And foredooms his own with his house's fall

604

Sloth kills his kith, his kin, his home destroys
Even as by slow degrees he his own destruction sires

605

Being slow, forgetful, slothful and sleepy is a junk-ride
Headed straight to sink in a shock-tide

606

There are those who undeserving gains come by
But the slothful never catch the good earth's kindly eye

The laggard is berated by his friends first then by the world
As by his sloth to his doom he is hurled

608

Sloth reduces a family of noble folk to serfs
Of those who have been its foes and worse

609

But if—some hope!—a sluggard give up his ways
Himself and his household from ruin he saves

610

The king who knows no sloth has under his foot
The world upon which once a mighty god stood

Chapter 62

THE STRENUOUS LIFE

611

Let not defeat be a fear, king, nor defeatism a habit of mind
Facing a hard task with grit you will triumph find

612

Choosing action over inaction, effort over despair
Is what the world applauds; do not fear—dare!

613

Wanting to help others is a noble form of pride
But to indulge it you cannot amble, you need to stride!

614

If you want to be of use, you've got to look sharp, be strong
Giving a weakling a battle axe would be both useless and wrong

615

He who shuns pleasure to find joy in right effort
Is for the needy a stout pillar of support

616

Striving for the good, good fortune does increase
Not striving so, ensures its decrease

617

Two sisters, Misfortune and Fortune, rule human living
The first embraces sloth, the other crowns striving

The ill-fortune of a low intelligence amounts to no disgrace
A high intelligence put to no account, is just a total waste
619
Should the fates seem unfair, do not despair
Hard work will your misfortune repair
620
Should luck desert you mid-battle when you need it, fear not!
Your efforts will dispense with luck and leave it asking: 'Whaaat?'

Chapter 63

FORTITUDE

621
When adversity strikes, blanch not but smile
And pass on to assured victory, agile
622
When sorrow engulfs you like a flood, drown not in it but think
The very thought that drowns in sorrow can make sorrow sink
623
Grief, dank and dreary, watches as we grieve
If you stay un-grieving, grieving grief will leave
624
Through stony high and thorny low the bullock plods its way
Meet each problem as it comes and you'll see it go away
625
When grief on grief mounted comes and yet your heart can't
crush
It'll call its work full wasted and leave in a rush
626
Those who didn't puff themselves up or sing about their wealth
Won't, if it is lost, go wailing and beating their breast
627
The human frame to agonize is pain's singular aim
Those who know this do not wail when pain is at its game

628

You cannot ever from sorrow hide
Take that reality in your stride

629

Who in happy days didn't in giddy joy explode
Won't in troubled times, sorrowing, implode

630

A step there is beyond detachment and this could sound weird—
Pain, when seen as pleasure, makes welcome what is feared

Chapter 64

THE GOOD MINISTER

631

Resources, a sense of time, right ways to oversee
Make the minister what a minister should be

632

Bold, un-relaxed in vigil, learned, wise
Being these makes a minister to his full scope rise

633

The minister who can split his foes, win angered friends back
And hold them, has that gift called 'knack'

634

The minister with sharp eyes sees
What will work, what won't
And, pondering them with calm, decrees:
'Do this like this and as for that—just don't'

635

The minister who knows what's right does and says it right
Aids the kingdom by his inner and 'over' sight

636

No problem's too big for a minister whose genius
'Native' as it's called, aided by the codes, is there to serve us

637

The minister who has mastered the manipulator's tract
Must yet find out how nature makes men act

638

The minister must from his seat say loud and ringing-clear
What he must, though a haughty king, and unwise, may refuse to
hear

639

The minister who intrigues under the monarch's very nose
Beats by far, by very far, his seventy crores of foes

640

The minister who relies on plans and lofty schemes alone
But forgets the ground stumbles on reality's stone

Chapter 65

POWER OF SPEECH

641

Of gifts that gifted ministers have the gift of the gifted tongue
Stands first, for on that one gift great schemes are hung

642

A minister's speech needs to guard against inaptness
For make or break it can, a kingdom's fate, no less

643

Only that speech is called a hit
Which has people rueing, 'I missed it!'

644

A speech must be within the entire audience's reach
So that each listener takes home the minister's praise to preach

645

Speak not that which a speaker on the other side
Can question, dispute or deride

646

Speak so as not to another's view tear apart
And the other side's wise thoughts embrace with all your heart

647

In words strong, in recall strong, strong in every thought
If you are these, defeat you the other side cannot

648

Minister, if your well-knit thoughts make a strong case
The world will your words with eagerness embrace

649

He who has not two thoughts to utter—or to mutter—straight
Will spin two thousand words to show how his head's laden with
weight

650

If what you have learnt, you cannot to others convey
You are the scentless flower that could as well be hay

Chapter 66

THE MORAL LAW

651

Help helps the helper and the helped
Helping others the helper's helping hand is also held

652

Do that and that alone which furthers good and good alone
And thereby save yourself from evils known and unknown

653

Should great deeds be your aim, from small deeds refrain
Shun deeds that put your name to risk, deeds that glory drain

654

No matter if troubles surround you, put your nerves to strain
You're safe if on the right path your sights you train

655

Do nothing, nothing whatever, that your soul will reprove
If you have sinned you have sinned but now—exit that groove!

656

Who would not do anything, anything whatever
To bring food to a hungering mother?
But pause if what you do, good souls deem wrong
Refrain, for even that filial act may to wrong belong

657

Far better, far better it is, to sink in virtuous poverty
Than stink in the slime of ill-gained prosperity

658

Those that do wrong and not care they do wrong
May sneer now but watch! Their happy days won't last long

659

What's got through guilt with guilty tears will go
What's lost though honestly got will be back—ergo!

660

For the king to seek his kingdom's gain through falsehood and
deceit
Is to pour water into an unfired pot believing it'll retain it

Chapter 67

THE EFFICIENT ACT

661

What a minister needs—in fact, all he needs—is strength of mind
A mind that knows what it wants; the rest is best left undefined

662

The wise say to the king:
'What's a no-go please forego, what's no-good expel
That to your subjects peace will bring
And all ill-doing repel'

663

Announce a scheme after it is done and not a day before
For an undone scheme can undo you, yours and more

664

Easy it is to speak, easy to lecture and preach
But hard, so very hard, the preached goals to reach

665

Kings respect and people praises shower
On those great persons who show thinking's power

666

As people think so can they accomplish
If they have the will to realize their wish

Being Politic

667

Great strength of mind and purpose can dwell in a poor frame
Go not by looks: the chariot wheel's linchpin has no fame

668

When decided upon with a clear mind the undertaking launch
Every obstacle surmount, unsleeping, every opposition staunch

669

Troubles will surround you but you must stay steadfast
Doing what's tough but right takes a fast to a repast

670

Those who possess power—and power in turn possesses
Don't charm the world
Which values those whose work their pelf surpasses
And who keep their egos furled

Chapter 68

THE OFFENSIVE

671

Deliberations must end in decision
Else they are a ramble
Decide after due reflection
And after that—act, not amble

672

Some operations there are that, so to say, must hatch
But others need asperity and dispatch
Sleep, if you like, over matters time can take care of
But those needing promptitude don't you put off!

673

Where the road forward is open, seize it at once
Where it is not, don't freeze, find other ones

674

Ignored, a duty and a foe with fire compare
Remember, even one ember, neglected, can flare

675

Means, men, moment, map and method
Consider well these five before to war you head

676

What your effort will entail, encounter, lose or make
Consider well before that journey you undertake

677

Before setting forth be humble enough to consult
Those who know the effort and can gauge its likely result

678

One perfect act its successor act helps picture
As one trained elephant another helps capture

679

Friends are a wealth, as the saying goes
But a greater wealth are foes of foes

680

'Our king defeated? No way,' they say
'We'd rather he sues for peace'
Knowing this, at close of day
The king bites his lip, bends his head and says to his foe, 'Please!'

Chapter 69

THE ENVOY

681

Some things an envoy just has to be—
Of nature, sweet; by birth, noble; in manner, refined
When he is these three
He will please the prince to whom he is assigned

682

Devoted loyalty, mastery of political lore, gift of the sifted word—
These three make an envoy fit to speak for his lord

683

The envoy bearing his king's firm word
Must strike his host as a man to be heard

684

Innate as well as acquired knowledge and grace—
If these three he has, let him as envoy proceed apace

685

Measured speech, void of grating words, will please
The prince and his own king's credit increase

686

Who knows much, speaks well and is of fearless eye
Is the one, witty and nimble, to make a good envoy

687

Who knows courtesies due, the time and place for things
And keeps those in view is a good envoy for kings

688

Who is in conduct never in error, in court never resourceless
Brave ever, and truthful is as an envoy priceless

689

Who bears his king's message must be worthy of his mandate
Must not by oversight or worse say that which will ruin it

690

Who conveys his king's message with verve and with vim
Should know—and not mind—that death will therefore stalk him

Chapter 70

DANGERS OF THE PALACE

691

The warming fire soothes; too close, it scorches
A king's glance now warms, now torches

692

If you do not covet what the monarch himself does prize
He will himself with generous love your station surprise

693

Suspicion, grey and grim, ever rules the royal breast
'Why, how, him or—him?' is a king's constant quest
So, never let the royal mind harbour doubt
For once in, doubt will never go out

694

Whisper not nor exchange smiles with friends before kings
Royalty misconstrues such normal, harmless things

695

Kings secrets whisper and kings secrets hear
Don't try overhearing them even just for fun
But if the king himself asks you to come near
Hear him in silence and to your work return

696

Sense the right propitious time and the right royal mood
Then say the needed word at the right royal sign to get the right royal 'Good!'

697

The royal ear likes to hear what's called the 'pleasant nothing'
Do not that innocent pastime begrudge him
But never speak idly, meaninglessly, to the king
Even though welcome to him it might seem
Matters that further his interest, of course,
Are always his—and so your—favourite discourse!

698

The king may be your kin, younger kin as well
But that is irrelevant
He's 'Protector of All who in his Kingdom Dwell'
Just remember that covenant

699

Be you ever so close never regard yourself immune
From royal ire which has no time for the old familial tune

700

Thinking 'Oh, we've known each other forever' do not presume
That court etiquette will such familiarity subsume

Chapter 71

KNOWLEDGE OF INDICATIONS

701

Who by reading signs and silent faces can prophecy
Is a gem of rare waters in this earth bound by the sea

702

Who can read the minds of men and of women
Is to be likened to the gods in heaven

Being Politic

703

Who by your face can tell your life's story
Calls for a gift from you, its conservatory

704

Who reads by signs and our future tells
May look like us but is something else

705

If seeing eyes see signs but see not signs' news
Of what use are they, of all our organs, of what use?

706

As a crystal mirror shows up whatever is beside it
The face pictures all that in the soul is writ

707

Be it joy or be it rage
The face is its foremost gauge

708

If you want to know a mind and reach the thoughts it holds
All you need is to see its face to know what it enfolds

709

Nothing matches the eye that beams both love and hate
To make you rise to its double bait

710

Ask the wise, 'How can we know what x, y, z feel?'
And they'll say, 'Watch their eyes, their eyes alone, will all reveal'

Chapter 72

THE COUNCIL CHAMBER

711

Minister, if you have a clear mind (as you should)
When you speak in council
Sense, first, your listeners' mood
And then select such words as will
Weave your thought into their natural bent
So that your message gets well and truly sent

Gauge your listeners' individual and collective mind
And then proceed to let your thoughts and words unwind

713

If you are ignorant about the council's sense
Your words will not work with it; they'll sound dense

714

Before the enlightened show your mind's bright spark
Before the blank, show yourself too to be as much in the dark

715

Speak only after the grey-with-age have had their say
Culture requires you exclaim, 'Me speak before you, sir? No way!'

716

To lose one's hold on speech and slip before the learned wise
Is very like the slithering slip from which you cannot rise

717

Those who know the art of using words aright
Know why the words of the learned ones always shine so bright

718

To speak high and wise to one who already knows
Is to try to irrigate grown grain standing in ripe rows

719

Those who speak well to Councils of the Good should never
Speak to Councils of the Ill, even in error

720

Like spreading nectar on the ground that can't taste
Is speaking to the strangers—a total waste

Chapter 73

DREAD NOT THE COUNCIL

721

Minister, when with pure intent
You use good words in council
Be sure to its natural bent
You attune your verbal skill

722

They are called learned who having learned what they have
learned
Can share their learning in right words with the learned

723

The rare one can be found who'll face death without flinching
But not one who will face the council without quaking

724

Speak up for what you've learned in words strong and good
But learn up what those from life have understood

725

Only if to relevant texts you have your mind applied
Will the council say to you, 'Well replied!'

726

Your learning's quite useless if you can't face the council
As your sharp sword's useless if you can't make your kill

727

A sword in a hermaphrodite's hand is a waste of sharpened steel
So learning in a nervous mind is lost to the council's weal

728

Whatever you have learned is learning unemployed
If in the council's chamber it has not been deployed

729

If those who have learned a thing or two yet, before the council,
quake
They the very next rank after unlearned take

730

If the 'learned' don't strike the council as 'well read'
Then, for that chamber, they might as well be dead

Chapter 74

THE GOOD NATION

731
In produce unfailing, unceasing in the raising of wealth
That land of good people is a nation in good health
732
Where people seek a share in the land's elevation
Where disasters are few and far apart, we have a nation
733
Where disregarding burdens it pays the king his portion
And keeps the state in money, we have a nation
734
Where hunger, illness and enmities cause no perturbation
That land, that happy land, is a nation
735
Where factions don't splinter life, strife brings no desolation
Where murderous hordes don't plague the king, we have a nation
736
Which an enemy neither dare invade nor trifle with its peace
And where, even in times of woe, its produce will increase
Is the best definition
Of an ideal nation
737
Where rain brings and springs spread water without limitation
Where mountains green and forts guard, that is a nation
738
Where health, wealth, fertility, security and jubilation
These five gems are found there we have a nation
739
Where the land increases its yields with its own affirmation
And not by others' mediation we have a nation
740
Where all this obtains and more but satisfaction
Sir, inner satisfaction
The king does not provide we do not have a nation
Sir, we do not have a true nation

Chapter 75

THE FORT

741
The fort sends the king forth to smash his foes
And shelters his subjects from raining arrows

742
A forest thick with bough and shade, a forecourt, a hill and a moat
Around it complete the form and function of a fort

743
High, wide, tough and unbreachable, these four a fort must be
As palladium of the kingdom's power, guarantor of its security

744
The fort should be wieldy, not too large to guard
Against attackers who must despair 'Oh, this wall's so hard!'

745
'Impregnable', yes, the fort should be—everyone knows that
But it should host its brave garrison with a first rate commissariat

746
The fort's repute at the end of the day rests not on walls and
munitions
But on its garrison's pluck against the foe's machinations

747
A fort should first be proof against the gambit called 'surround'
Next, far-flying darts and sabotage by the invisible underground

748
The fort should be such as to frustrate the foe
And become the attacker's ultimate woe

749
The fort should halt the foe at first sight
With its in-built glory and might

750
Be its walls ever so stout the fort is one stone-heap
If its command is in weak hands and the garrison's become sheep

Chapter 76

THE EXCHEQUER

751

This we must hand to means
There's nothing in the world like it
Nothing nearly since
Time from mud made the hominid
Prosperity alone
Makes of mere men persons who can matter
Who earn and own
The former to make the latter

752

Those without means the world disdains
On those with, praise rains

753

Wealth is a lamp that travels far spreading its lustrous glow
Darkness dispelling, notice compelling, it shines on its owner's
brow

754

If earned honestly
And used modestly
Wealth can elevate
Its owner's social state

755

But wrenching wealth off another is foul
If you do that you are a ghoul

756

The king's wealth is from three sources a just portion:
One, his inheritance
Two, produce's due fraction
And three, war's remittance

757

Wealth as a giving purse
Can foster grateful love
So it can, in a sense, play nurse
And a noble purpose serve

Watching like kings tuskers fight from a safe high vantage
Men of wealth can view battles secure—a great advantage

759

No weapon of war nears the lethal weapon called wealth
Let your foe feel your money's steel and its razor's tensile strength

760

On those who abundant wealth have made
The other two—virtue and love—gladly wait

Chapter 77

THE ARMY

761

In all its arms complete
In strength of heart replete
Of proud and stately bearing
Of the wounds of war unfearing
In conquest daring, quick and bold
Such an army, for the king, outweighs its weight in gold

762

When tough is the foe, rough the task, terrain and timing snarled
Depend on veteran soldiers, of knee and knuckle gnarled

763

Mice miming the rushing wave can let forth a micey yell
Let them! One snort of the Great Naag will send them all
scurrying to hell

764

Unstained by defeat and by purchase un-seduced
The old sire-and-son regime stays strong and un-subdued

765

That is a force, true mighty force it is, whose ranks stand in order
Un-scattered and un-scared by the threats of the enemy's horde

766

The valorous advance in true warlike pride
They make the enemy host cower and hide

Step by measured step the force proceeds apace
Expecting blows, the enemy horde to face

768

Even if in bold offence or strong defence untried
The force that is well-formed and drilled will the battle bestride

769

The force should not have to cope
With a chief who is a dope
Should not have to lose its sleep
Over stingy upkeep
And be forced to ask, 'Why is
No one seeing to supplies?'

770

An army's soldiers may be the world's best
But in its leaders' merit lies its biggest asset

Chapter 78

VALOUR

771

Those who stood before my chief are now tomb-rock
So, dare him only if you wish to join that flock stock

772

No part of valour it is, no part
To send an arrow into a scampering hare's heart
To train it, though, at an elephant's brain
Is brave even if trained in vain

773

On the battlefield ferocity is your weapon
But to the fallen foe kindness you must open

774

They stand face to face
One with trunk upraised
The other with cold grimace
The elephant trumpets, crazed

The soldier whirls and hurls
His gleaming javelin
As the pachyderm's blood curdles
The soldier knows it's in
The four-legged one will charge again
Charge again he will ·
The soldier feels a pang of pain
But will not be counted ill
He finds a dart that's pierced his side
'Baley!' he shouts, 'I'm armed!' plucks and flings
It at the menacing hide
He is not made of earthly things
That man, he is not made of earthly things
775

The ready-to-die braveheart
If hit by a spear
Won't even let his eyes smart
Lest his life appear dear
776

The fighting brave deem those days a waste
When their limbs no war wounds taste
777

For those that value fame no sign can more define
Than the warrior's gem-clasp, of deathless guts a sign
778

For the battle-borne no song tugs as battle's ancient gong
Royal yes or royal no, they'll fly to that song headlong
779

Who fails if in 'do or die' one dies?
Dying with a winful doing vies
780

No mourning is as meet, no grief as honour-borne
As a king's lament for his brave soldier, gone

Chapter 79

FRIENDSHIP

781
If you want to know what the world means by 'a hard thing to
find'
Try to find friends who'll guard you against ill and your good to
their's bind

782
Friendships, good and wise, grow like the waxing moon that grows
Those that are neither, shrivel like—you guessed it—the waning
moon does

783
The more you read a book you love the more you want to re-read
it
The more you love a friend the more that friend want to meet

784
Friendship's for laughter, yes, laughter is life's tonic
But the friend who reproves your wrong also gives you physic

785
Any two beings can think and work together
But only true friends can feel like and with the other

786
The smile that smiles to another smile is but a veneer
That smile's a smile which embraces the heart when two come
near

787
Friendship keeps; it keeps you from ruin and keeps your virtue too
In times of sorrow it weeps as you weep which is why it is called
true

788
As swift as the arm that saves one's vesture from slipping
Is the help of a friend when it comes at the moment of reckoning
Or to say
It another—franker—way
As fleet as my hand that halts the sarong's shaming slide
Comes timely help to save one's imperilled pride

789

Friendship has a seat and that seat a function:
To support each other at life's every junction

790

The friendship that says 'this gesture I have made'
Or 'that favour he has done' is not friendship but trade

Chapter 80

FORMING FRIENDSHIPS

791

Friendships are not deals to be signed and sealed
And after some shock, broken and repealed
Friendships, in fact, are formed not made
Formed to last through life's light-and-shade

792

Befriending one you have not known in testing times
Can cause you grief; so be wise and change tack, betimes!

793

How does his mind work, from where does he hail
Does he have dark corners, hidden friends who'd better be in jail
Find out these things about him from others who know him
But once assured, trust him, trust him to trust's overflowing rim

794

If the man be well-descended, of guilt and shame aware
Consider no cost too great for him, no thought too rare to share

795

This is hard, I know, but befriend the one who's tough
With you when you go wrong, not smoothing what's rough

796

Can ruin contain a good? Strangely, yes—as a measuring staff
To know who stands by you to the hilt and who not even by half

797

Wisdom in its wisdom rules:
Move you away from fools!

Some thoughts stunt your soul, shun them by saying: 'Out!'
Some 'friends' stymie you, stun them by dubbing them 'lout!'
799
'Friends' who, at the Testing Hour, fled you
Burn you up when, at the Crossing Hour, you your life review
800
To stainless men with tenacity adhere
Don't let the worthless come anywhere near!

Chapter 81

FAMILIARITY

801
'The old familiar' is friendship's oldest friend
Where trust, rubbed by use, gleams like an old door-knob
Opening to rooms where speech and silence blend
The known is shared with laughter, the unknown with a throb
Where doors are not bolted just secured with a latch
Where taut and smooth relax into age's soft burrows
Where hope becomes dreamy as faith and failure match
Where love its freedom and fun its limit knows
There, that 'old familiarity', pazhaimai,
Draws softly the 'us' from the once-high ruling 'I'
802
The trust in intimacy gives friendship its form
A duty to that trust true friendship must inform
803
If friendship does not to familiarity respond
It forfeits the beauty of that bond
804
It is friendship's genius
To be both measured and spontaneous
805
If a friend shows lack of thought or care for your feelings
Put it down to old familiarity, don't brood 'Oh! He has grown new
wings'

806

Friendship abandons not a friend who might cross
Absent-minded or mindfully familiarity's laws

807

And if it transpires 'an old familiar' from friendship's trust strays
Friendship has room within, and sense, to see he comes right back
and stays

808

The day, the testing day, one you have loved and guarded
From others' slander and regarded
Dearer than your own repute
Turns his back on you, don't despair—be mute
And count that day a day of grace
When with peace you are face to face

809

The friendship that never fails
Our friendless world hails

810

Those who are not friends, 'foes' one might even call them
Even those, to 'old familiarity' give welcome

Chapter 82

EVIL FRIENDSHIP

811

Evil men with honeyed words to win friendship's hand attempt
Does one give that evil favour? No! One treats it with contempt

812

Let selfish friends know you know their evil ends
You can do without them on life's blind bends

813

Those who friendship in gain's scales weigh
Say, 'I'll please you as much as you can pay'

814

The wild flying steed is great to be on
But in the hour of need? It's gone!

815

Better not gain than gain the gainless trying to pass for gain
Petty minds, sly and small, calling it 'gain' will sell you pain

816

A wise man on the other side is your gain
A fool on this, your bane

817

Ten million times more is there benefit in a foe
Than in a nitwit of a sniggering beau

818

To those who say they are your friendship's prop
Ask, 'Is that so, indeed?' and then the prop silently drop

819

Those whose deeds with their words don't agree
Don't even in dreams permit entry

820

Those who hug you in your parlour then stab you from the stage
Do not in any friendly act, talk, or business engage

Chapter 83

UNREAL FRIENDSHIP

821

Don't be the anvil which 'friends' beat with glee
To burnish their base metal hoping you won't see

822

Friends whose minds are fickle as women's are wont to be
Can change colour before you say, 'One, two, three'

823

High learning and the arts are about culture
But being good of heart, quite another picture

824

Those whose pinched hearts don't stretch but whose smiles do
Keep as far as you can from you

825

If you think different from the other, shall I say, chap
Don't trust words to bridge the gap

The foe's simmering thought hides in glimmering word
But it will soon be out and be clearly 'eard

827

The enemy's word bends as supple as his bow
Its poison tip can get you in one whizzing go

828

As his palms come together
They could a weapon harbour
Beware, likewise, of an enemy's tears
They're a front for the mind that leers

829

Those who smile and smile and then beguile
Should receive at your hands rejection's fatal projectile

830

Don't shy from returning wily smile for wily smile
And plot between your smiles your own smiling wile

Chapter 84

FOLLY

831

Folly it is, its very height, your dice so to toss
That it turns undoubted gain to assured loss

832

Folly it is, the very height of folly, to lust after an enterprise
Which beyond your calling lies

833

The lout of all shame devoid
Is of duties, compassion and care—paranoid!

834

Folly's no imbecile; it can act learned and be vile
The virtues it teaches it breaches all the while

835

'Live with folly this life and then with pain in seven'
Is a tenet given to us by an ever-watchful heaven

836

If for your task you are unsuited or untrained
You will to failure and worse be chained

837

The cash-rich fool spreads for foes a repast
Leaving his poor friends to fast

838

Fools brimming with cash and dimwits with drink
Act exactly alike and alike do they sink

839

Befriending fools is not a bad thing
For dumping them relief will bring

840

As one with muddied feet can make his bed a bog
A fool joining the wise can dim their light in fog

Chapter 85

IGNORANCE

841

Among the world's many wants one that takes the palm
Is that which does real and lasting harm:
The want of knowledge and knowledge of that want
All other wants the world can get by with, but this it just can't

842

When the fool gifts something he gifts from his fooldom
The gifted one thanks his stars for the fool being so dumb

843

Beating the agonies which come from foes
Are those which fools add to life's woes

844

The stupid are stupid for the wisdom they claim
And by that act their un-wisdom declaim

845

The stupid are stupid for pretending they know
Thereby doubt on their intentions sow

Vain, the draping of limbs to privacy disposed
When a shameless mind, stark naked, is exposed

847

The loss of inherited lore
Makes the loser a boor

848

Needing but not heeding counsel marks off a fool
And plunges his whole life in ignorance's stagnant pool

849

The blind of mind are blind for they refuse to 'see'
To think the blind of eye are blind is great stupidity
For they do see in their own inner way
What we miss in the glare of the day

850

Who would say of what exists that it does not?
And those who do, are said to be of the demon sort!

Chapter 86

HOSTILITY

851

To life's simple joys the hostile mind is averse
And infects each living thing with its thoughts perverse

852

No harm in holding to your view, in being to your own self true
But there's great harm, very great harm, in harming those
differing from you

853

Enmity is an ill, a grievous ill, to shun
Shunning it, the world's praise is won

854

If you choose not to hate those who grate on your nerves
You'll buy peace thereby with joy's huge reserves

855

If you have conquered enmity
You've stilled the threat to equanimity

856
If you harbour hostility
You're tempting mortality
857
Enmity blinkers if it does not blind
Us to all greatness in humankind
858
'Move you away from all enmity'
Does that sound trite?
It isn't, really, try it!
And save yourself from a life of adversity
859
Those two are twinned—ill-fortune and enmity
In good times all seems great, in bad—a calamity
860
Enmity plays misfortune
Friendliness the other, happier, tune

Chapter 87

HATRED

861
When your foe stands taller, retreat
When of lesser size, don't dissemble—defeat!
862
Unwarmed by love unbacked by strength
Your leap will have no length
The enemy will exult in joy
'None by way of kin he has, nor any kith in his cause to employ'
863
'The man is dim,' the foe exclaims, 'and what's more, he has no
vim
So easy, so awful easy it is to flatten him!'
864
With temper out-blown, his every secret known
He is the easiest prey out of or even in his zone

865

In means wanting, of values bereft
To good and bad, quite dead
He is by his own failings left
To be to piteous failure fed

866

The more he lusts and the more he rages the more likeable he
For you won't often find both 'virtues' in one and the same enemy

867

If an 'undesirable' offers help in your enterprise
Buy his hate, not his help, and save your work—even at a price!

868

When no virtues adorn but faults becloud a man
His foes benefit from staying as far from him as they can

869

If dim of wit, of valour slim, he gives his enemy joy
He thereby gifts him triumph as his very toy

870

Those who do not trounce in war men in war unskilled
Forfeit that minor honour in battle's guild

Chapter 88

ENMITY

871

Close your soul's door to enmity
Not to be opened even in jest or thoughtless levity

872

Of the sharp-eyed one whose 'plough' is a bow, fear
Near the sharp-tongued one whose 'plough' is a word, don't dare!

873

The miserable wretch who has no friend
But makes foes galore
Does not know friendlessness can end
But a foe is for evermore

874

The world feels secure with one who turns foe to friend
And thus shows 'foeness' can end

875

If you have no ally—no surprise there!—and face not one foe but two
Make of one an instant friend and watch the other rue

876

When luck sinks low think not: 'Is he friend or foe?'
Equidistant stay from both, till things are as before

877

Your woes keep from your foes and from friends as well
Let no one your weakness sense or your misery smell

878

View well your road then launch upon it strong
Looking the enemy in the eye sound your victory gong

879

Take out the thorn when still young, its nib soft and slender
Left to grow it will draw blood its point no longer tender

880

Those that halt not the foe in his tracks
Count as dead for being so very lax

Chapter 89

THE ENEMY WITHIN

881

Shade cools, water quenches thirst
That is their nature, calling, first
But both another role can play
And harm instead of love portray
So too with kith and so-called kin—
They can do you good, they can do you in

882

When armed with spears foes appear
Their purpose is all too clear

Being Politic　　　　　95

But they can disguise themselves like kin
Saying 'Hey ho' and 'How've things been?'
That's when you must be aware
Of the need in life to take due care
883

Beware of the hate that deep inside lies
Like a potter's sharp knife it knows how to slice
884

When enmity sucks at a mind in the dark
Kin plan the bite that does not bark
885

Hate in kin
Works like a toxin
Hidden
To work unbidden
886

Hate within kin who once were in and now are anything but
Will seep through your door; do what you will to keep it firmly
shut
887

In a lidded dish its lid and dish are not one thing but two
So is one hate-filled household a broken up thing too
888

Like a file with its incisors works to pare down gleaming gold
Hate's sharp teeth can wear down a sturdy old household
889

Slight as a split in a sesame seed
Insider hate may be
Yet to do its lethal deed
Nothing can match its potency
890

Home life for those who cannot concordance make
Is like having for sole neighbour, in a hole, a snake

Chapter 90

NOT OFFENDING THE GREAT

891
Slight not those in power or 'the mighty' as they're called
If you don't want to be blacklisted or worse, be blackballed
892
It never is good policy to cross the mighty ones
They are strong, you are not, at their will the nation runs
They may do things you can't excuse
But they hold office, you hold views
They have the power and the will
To make of your major move a minor kill
893
The mighty ones, let's face it, have the power to ruin us
To shut our eyes and plug our ears to this simple fact will be
ruinous
894
To do such deeds as could harm the mighty ones in power
Is—let me be blunt—
To start a hunt
And to invite Death to make this very moment his hour
895
Wherever the king-defiers flee, howsoever they scatter
They will get served for sure to Death on a platter
896
Fires, real blazing ones, are with danger fraught
But still are nothing compared to a king's raging wrath
897
Gifts lose all meaning, wealth too and renown
If the king of the day chooses on you to frown
898
Your virtues and your valour may well be sky-high
If the king does not esteem them you might as well—die!
899
And yet, yes, and yet, let me also grant you this
There is such a thing as fearlessness

When men of high repute take on an unjust king
He is bound to fall, that king, and look a sad little thing
900
Will wealth and power, then, to such a ruler be of no avail?
If the virtuous and the truly great oppose him, they are bound to
fail

Chapter 91

BEING LED BY WOMEN

901

As you embark on a new, noble venture
And your wife, tensed up, says, 'Don't'
Ask her to relax, not rupture
Fortune can't be told, 'I won't'
902
If your time is meant for others don't disgrace
Yourself as 'prisoner of the wife's embrace'
903
If you're at your wife's and not your duty's service
You'll be seen for what you are: a house-mouse unfit for high office
904
Even though in deeds heroic
And on battlefields stoic
If at home a spineless slave
He will never earn the title 'brave'
905
If, wretched he, before his wife is atremble
He will before other tasks quail and dissemble
906
Though king-like his lifestyle and royal his means
The man ruled by his wife's hand, his station demeans
907
Be he the 'mighty one' and she the 'so modest'
When might is slave to modesty we can guess the rest

908

If your wife's high-browed wish is law
Friends' needs and good causes are but straw

909

Your work, wealth and, why, wellness as well
If wife-rule's your fate, in her will, dwell

910

If you let your ideas fly and in ideas make your world
The taunt of 'wife-servitude' won't on you be hurled

Chapter 92

WOMEN

911

When an armlet sways and sweet words twirl
Around you, don't go all dovey dove
Those 'sweet' acts come from a harsh world
That wants your purse, not love

912

When sweet words masking bitter needs snuggle up to you
Remember the whys and hows of it and swiftly bid adieu

913

In a darkened room on a corpse outstretched you'd stumble
The same it is when with a whore you tumble!

914

Those who know the life of old-world grace
Will steer clear of all that brings with it disgrace

915

From the guiles and styles of tinsel wiles
Men who are wise will stay away miles

916

To the tactical tactility of the tactfully untactful
Men who are wise will not be useful

917

Those who by disgrace's embraces are held
Have never true grace beheld

918

Men in wisdom void treacherous love permit
They soil their name by crossing decorum's limit

919

Un-wisdom drives men to sink disgraced
In arms begemmed and gold clasps braced

920

That good-for-nothing, wine-bibbing, dice-throwing loon
The benighted befriends to his misfortune

Chapter 93

NOT DRINKING PALM WINE

921

The palm's sap no gain confers but loss
Repute with the bubbles bursts, prestige takes a toss

922

Keep off the draught, keep off, say, 'No sir!' and stay off it
It rips you, that thing does, trips and strips you, makes you a silly
twit

923

Making a mother grieve should be shame enough but elders too
Will scoff, 'Be off, you bib, go join the beggar queue'

924

And that lovely being, the village girl, will take fright
Fleeing, will pant 'I fear that drunk's very sight'

925

Of all the foolish things fools do, the absolute worst
Is paying up hard cash to cause themselves hurt

926

When you a deep sleep sleep, you're as good they say as dead
Instead of the palm's mind-numbing drink you could try poison
instead

927

The village elders call you 'sleepy-eye' and 'toddy boy'
You do not want, do you, to let that taunt get by

The bibber in a darkened room thinks he bibs unseen
E'en as the village dubs his hidden bibbing a double sin
929
Don't reason with one who gets each day well and truly drunk
You might as well look, lamp in hand, in the sea for a boat that
has sunk
930
If the sober one tries but once the drunken dunce to ape
He'll know at once the risk and from its grip escape

Chapter 94

GAMBLING

931
The fish wide-eyed swims into its fate when caught by the wiggling
bait
Do not, open-eyed, make that mistake, stop dead at gambling's
gate
932
Can a gambler who squanders a hundred for one
From a hundred lost days show one he has won?
933
The king who rolls and rolls the rolling dice
Pays in old gold and new, a very heavy price
934
Gaming is a slope you climb only to slide
From high to low in one swift glide
935
In dice, dice-room and dice-throwing
Who revel dreaming of gain, are paupers in the making
936
Gambling is twin to Misfortune and with her sister veils us
And then leads us, blindfolded, to an ugly terminus
937
Self-made renown and inherited estate
Both, in gambling homes, evaporate

938

Gambling grips with a vice-like grip the gambler's mind and soul
In both his fame and his purse it punches a gaping hole

939

Once of dicing you become a slave you are its slave forever
It devours your wealth, your learning, fame and even what you
wear

940

The gambler knows he wastes, knows he wastes away
Yet gambles on as some men do in a life that's had its day

Chapter 95

MEDICINE

941

Disease, say the books, comes from sources three
Led by wind, the other two in its lee
As one works or does not you get well or ill
Your purse to save or pay a heavy bill

942

Health has much to do with what and when and how you eat
Let what's inside you settle before you pile more and more on't

943

A healthy body'll stay healthy if you don't keep stuffing it up
Don't heap food on food; stop before you burp!

944

To 'eat well' is to not eat full or to eat too rich
Don't dump it in, your stomach's not a ditch
Eat joyously, not recklessly, for health is not for free
And never eat before you're truly hungry

945

Saying 'no' to more and eating what is right
Will keep all illness well out of sight

946

How much food would too much be and how much food just right
You've got to know if you're not to bow to illness' might

If you stop just before you reach your fill
Be sure you won't from eating fall ill
947
If you eat to the measure of hunger's fire
Not more, you will ill health defy
948
Physician sir! Only when of the disease, its cause and likely cure
you have insight
Then and then alone, go about setting it right
949
Physician sir, check the patient's strength of body and of mind
And the stage of the disease before you try its proper cure to find
950
These are vital to a cure: the patient of course, a sound doctor
The right remedy and the wary attendant—why, we almost forgot
her!

Chapter 96

NOBILITY

951
Only those line-bred to walk in virtue's way
Every act of theirs in their conscience weigh
952
Those that weigh word and deed in thought's even scale
Know by nascency what's what and never fail
953
To smile, to give, to speak the good and gracious word
Comes from being born to truth-telling and in it reared
954
Gold heaped up in tempting display
Will never one of high lineage sway
955
The granary may its grain forfeit, the coffer all its gold
Yet the honour of the exalted ones will never be sold

956

Firm-set in his ancestor's mores
The scion from the path never strays

957

A stain on one of noble birth is stark
As are on the moon, its craters deep and dark

958

If you happen a noble name to bear
Do not risk showing a lack of care

959

A plant reflects the soil which sends it forth
A word the mind in which it takes birth

960

To be esteemed as 'the good one'
You must all shaming deeds shun
To be held by people dear
You must all life revere

Chapter 97

HONOUR

961

Honour that which your own honour won't stain
That which may or will, you should just not entertain

962

Glory can be bought and sold
Painted lead can pass for gold
True honour knowing this well
Its glory refuses to sell

963

One day is a win, the next a washout
Kneel when you swell, rise up when knocked out

964

Hair scorned by their roots slip onto the ground
The mighty thus spurned by fortune are drowned

Howsoever high the 'high' man's height
One mean act and he's in a very sorry plight

966

Go not with the scoffing cynic, nor for his approval wait
His tribe, un-praised, with the gods has no date

967

Go not with the cynic for he is well despised
Better be dead than with the likes of him be spied

968

For the highly honoured when honour goes all goes
And for vile flesh life has no drug, salve, balm or dose

969

The forest ox, its tuft shorn, loses the will to live
All honour torn, the once-honoured would rather go down the
sieve

970

Who, honour-shorn, refuse to live another day
The world applauds for showing life another way

Chapter 98

GREATNESS

971

A mind that is alive lights up one's life
Shut that light out and you cease to be alive

972

Each into this world like the other comes
Then by degrees the other becomes

973

After all has been seen and done
Who finally is great?
Not, for sure, the mean of mind
Of however high estate
But he of the lowly kind
Whose honour is his own

974
As a woman stays strong as she stays true
Greatness to greatness must accrue

975
If by nature he's truly great
His deeds with greatness will reverberate

976
Those that are not to great deeds inclined
Will never their lives to greatness bind

977
The powerful and the great
Are two very different things
When power crowns the unregenerate
Its haughty insolence stings

978
The great know how to bow, the haughty never kneel
They strut, they preen, hollow head to heavy heel

979
Greatness has no vanity
And meanness no civility

980
Greatness a neighbour's shame will hide
Meanness, spread it far and wide

Chapter 99

PERFECTION

981
Being good is to the good more than doing good
It is being true to the duties of humanhood

982
Being good is about being good within
Not about being Lord or Lady Clean

983
Goodness stands on five tenets' force
Love, modesty, empathy, grace and—truth, of course

984

An iron law says, 'You shall not kill'
A golden one: 'Do not speak ill'

985

The mighty stoop to conquer
When they can smite to win
The biggest triumphs occur
When haughty pride's reined in

986

A noble soul is he whom defeat does not sear
When dealt by one wholly inferior

987

What among nobility's traits ranks first?
Helping those who've caused you hurt

988

The noble one if poor is noble nonetheless
Lack of earthly goods brings him no disgrace

989

Nobility is a sea no tide or tempest troubles
No ill-wind turns, no ill-fate ruffles

990

The bounteous earth will scarce survive
If on its vast estate virtue cannot thrive

Chapter 100

COURTESY

991

If those who need you can reach you
You are among the world's courteous few

992

To be born to grace and that birth not disgrace
By meanness is to dignity embrace

993

'Like' and 'same' are not the same, not the same by far
It's how two men feel, not look, that makes them on par

994

The good-natured and generous, those two
The world acclaims as 'born to virtue'

995

Do not scorn others at play or in friendly jest
Nor even in rightful rage

996

If noble souls did not hold the world aloft
It would come very quickly to nought

997

Sharp as a saw's fine teeth are those called 'bright'
But their souls are dead wood untouched by love's light

998

The mean provoke, they infuriate
But the courteous, wisely, don't retaliate

999

To smile the smile that comes from kindness' way
Is to dispel the dark that envelops the earth's dire day

1000

Milk will curdle in a soiled pot
So will wealth in a miser's vault

Chapter 101

WEALTH WITHOUT BENEFACTION

1001

A hoarder of wealth from which no joy is had, no hunger fed
Is useless, fit to be pronounced dead

1002

Those who don't share their wealth knowing well its worth
Are spooks, not men, and lose all right to human birth

1003

A burden, no less, on this earth
Are those who prize but gold
And spurning honour's worth
Succumb to lucre's hold

1004

Someone no one loves and will never miss
Has, at close of light, none he can call his

1005

They beggar themselves who living in their mint
Neither love nor share its glow and its glint

1006

Closed fists that do not know the joy of giving
And pinch-tight hearts wealth will one day sting

1007

With time, beauty will begin to fade
So will wealth, when it is not shared

1008

A poison tree, fruit-laden, is lonely in the village mart
A miser, wealth-laden, has no place in a people's heart

1009

Of all fine feelings bereft, an unkind, uncaring cash-pot
The hoarder will leave his stash behind, unused, to rot

1010

Like a raincloud suddenly gone dry
The wealthy can find his fortune say a fearful bye

Chapter 102

SHAME

1011

Modesty is one thing, shame another
One comes from virtue, from sin the other

1012

To feel hunger, know modesty is common instinct
But repugnance to evil—now *that* makes one distinct

1013

As life finds its tenement in a body
Virtue finds in conscience its abode

1014

Without the voice that says, 'For shame, don't!'
Pride is by infamy stripped, by honour scorned

To keep one's honour is on one's own repute to roam
To save another's shame is to live in virtue's home

The fence of shame guards all that virtues teach
And helps one, thus guarded, higher realms to reach

One may give up one's life for the sake of one's honour
Never one's honour to court in some shameless corner, dishonour

To be shameless when all around you know shame
Is to make virtue recoil from your very name

To break codes is to lose your place 'midst kin
To break honour is to forfeit your worth within

Those without a conscience knock about life's stage
As alive as the stringed-puppets bobbing in their cage

Chapter 103

CITIZENSHIP

1021

No better citizenship there is or, indeed, greatness
Than serving fellow-beings in their distress
1022

Unslackening in good works and uncompromising in wisdom
It is the people, simple men and women, who enrich the kingdom
1023

When the good citizen says, 'I'll serve my people, raise them high'
Divinity girds him, fits him, with public servants to vie
1024

The good citizen acts not counting pain or cost
In a flash with neither time nor target lost
1025

The world acclaims and citizens proclaim a friend
Him who makes blameless service his end

1026

More than serving people one's born among
No higher valour is known in story or in song

1027

As the valiant hero takes up the brunt of furious battles
The good citizen takes up his people's various struggles

1028

The proud and the lazy can never a family rear
Self-indulgence is a load the home cannot bear

1029

The public-minded citizen hides his griefs and sorrows
To give his benighted kin some hope for their tomorrows

1030

That citizenry is blighted and condemned to doom
Which has no strong hand to hold the roof over the room

Chapter 104

AGRICULTURE

1031

The world ventures over many fields, it tries one and then another
But returns again to the tasking plough as a child to its mother

1032

The ploughman axles the world, holds it firm for those
Who shrink from day-labour and farming's many woes

1033

He who toils to raise his food can be said to live by right
He who doesn't is a cringing parasite

1034

That monarch's reign extends long and far afield
Whose fertile pastures grain in bounty yield

1035

Ploughers do not ask but give with both hands filled
To those that ask, the bounty they have tilled

1036

If the ploughman were to fold his hands and let his tillage die
Sages and seers would see their great callings fly!

1037

There is after ploughing the next step called airing
One-fourth of the turned-up bulk must get that breathing

1038

A must after ploughing the soil is giving it manure
And after weeding and watering it, guarding it secure

1039

A field neglected is like a wife disdained
Be sure it will sulk and call you coarse-grained

1040

The hard-worked forbearing earth is amused
By those who wail, 'Poor me, I'm so ill-used'

Chapter 105

POVERTY

1041

Poverty's the worst of pains, the absolute worst
Its only rival is itself by its own self accursed

1042

Poverty loves to destroy
This world's and the next one's joy

1043

Want is poverty's second self, for it always is in want
Want of a better past to claim, a present that does not haunt

1044

Penury is blind to heredity, to noble line and grace
It makes the once-high speak very low, to their disgrace

1045

From that one source, poverty, spring ills that make things worse
More sorrow on sorrow grows, ill luck on old curse

1046

Good words, wise and true
If from the poor they come
Just don't get their due
In life's showy proscenium

1047

With one who has become poor, society won't relate
Why, poverty can even one's own mother separate

1048

Waking to a blighted dawn
In abject grief he bends
'Yesterday ground me down
Will today make amends?'

1049

A man may sleep through a flaming fire
But he can't rest a moment in poverty that's dire

1050

Who wants the poor at his doorstep to halt?
Who'll want to spend on their gruel and salt?

Chapter 106

MENDICANCY

1051

Ask unabashed when the askable come your way
If they do not oblige, it is not you who lose but they

1052

To ask for alms is also pleasure of a kind
If on asking gently a good response you find

1053

To ask for alms is, in a sense, an act of grace
If the gracious giver has kindliness on his face

1054

To seek alms can even bring a distinct joy
If the asking cannot, even in his dream, the giver annoy

1055

It is because alms-givers abide on this good earth
That alms-seekers claim to have in life some worth

1056

If you are lucky enough to find such noble men
Be sure your poverty is meant to end

1057
If you find alms-givers with no wrathful word or scorn
You are a joyous being though to begging born

1058
But for praying mendicants the world would be a sorry place
Where men like puppets bob about with a fixed wooden face

1059
If it were not for mendicants who graciously receive
Would alms-givers get noticed as 'the gracious ones that give'?

1060
The alms-seeker must in wrath not sway
His misery and pain say all he has to say

Chapter 107

LABOUR

1061
And yet, yes, and yet, all said and done a million times better it is
To not have to beg even those blessed with caring eyes

1062
May he, yes, may he who has so fashioned this world unjust
That men should have to beg, may he, like them, wander accurst

1063
Desperation, sheer, sharp and miserable, makes the poor
Decide, gulping their pride, to go knocking door by door

1064
When one who has not a place to lay his head says, 'Yes,
It's tough but, no, I won't beg,' he shows true excellence

1065
Thinner than thin though the thinned gruel may be
'Tis sweetest most for made of grains earned by me

1066
You risk being shooed and as a 'dirty beggar' cursed
If you as much as ask for water to slake a cow's thirst

1067
Of all the world's begging beggars I beg to beg just this one thing
From those who hoard their wealth in stealth, please, beg nothing

1068
Begging is a canoe, a light little thing she is
On hitting the rock 'No!' she just breaks and sinks
1069
The thought 'I must beg' is shattering enough
What's even worse is the prospect of a rebuff
1070
If asking for alms is asking for a kind of venom
Should giving that venom the alms-giver not envenom?

Chapter 108

BASENESS

1071
The base look just like us, just as we look like the base
And they resemble the devil, a fact we've got to face
1072
The base are luckier far than the other good kind
Not one care tugs their heart, not one regret, their mind
1073
The base are like—who else?—the gods!
They do as they please and when and face no odds
1074
When one who is base sees another who is vile
He will smart though he will also smile
1075
What on this earth can hold the base back?
Penal fear and the hope of gain in that very slack
1076
The base have, among many others, one notorious feature
Like the drum, they sound your secrets for everyone to hear
1077
The base one has sticky palms on which stick sticky grain
That will not drop until a mailed fist has pounded his brain
1078
The good render service for they feel others' pain
The base do so only when pressed like sugar cane

1079

If the base sees another well clothed, shod and turned out
He will in envy say, 'This man has an evil side, no doubt'

1080

The base is base and being base is base
But he does play this one good role
When he falls, like anyone else, on evil days
He sells himself to save his soul

Book III

BEING IN LOVE

Chapter 109

THE CELESTIAL MARRIAGE

1081

Tell me, are you a goddess?
You look like that gorgeous bird of changing hue
Gem-studded, you seem for other, not human, view
I swear, you have me witless

1082

As my eyes yours try
Foolishly to entangle
Unrivalled One, your sigh
Leaves me in a dangle

1083

Your eyes have done me in
Stolen my very breath
Till now I hadn't a clue a maiden
Could be my death

1084

She looks that simple, guileless soul
Of course, with form all soft and tender
But her goblet eyes that drink me whole
Are—what shall I say—plain murder

1085

Her glance is a shaft of light
Death's fatal spear
A fawn's tripping flight
A trident to strike fear!

1086

If only her brows would louvre her eyes
And their lids slat the glare
My heart's beat would cease to rise
And its aspiration to flare

1087

Eye-shields keep the elephant raged
From hurtling out of line
Satin coils twin globes cage
As, for play, they pine

Being in Love

1088

She steals all my strength—and how!
Out goes all vigour, all will to smite
My foe, relieved, blesses the brow
That fills my day, drains my night

1089

A fawn's limpid eyes she has
Her form is soft and supple
What need is there for the lovely lass
Her skin with jewels to couple?

1090

Sweet-tasting nectar of the palm
Wine, to derange, must on the tongue recline
But love, ah, can derange, disarm
If I my eye towards you, for just a moment, incline

Chapter 110

RECOGNITION OF THE SIGNS OF LOVE

1091

The first glance—this is sorcery, pure—
Makes me ill, the next brings its cure

1092

When she looked me in the face, half shade, half shine
I knew that more than half her love was mine

1093

When she looked at me and, blushing, looked down
Dew glistened on her love shoot's gentle crown

1094

I look at her, she focuses her eyes, serious-serious, on the ground
I look away, she looks up, smiling—an excuse has been found

1095

Just when she acts as if I simply don't exist
Love steals gently over her lips like a mist

1096

'Love, what's that?' she says, in her 'who're you?' act
But then her lips betray what is and what's not fact

1097

The searing words are high theatre scripted to insult
Him she loves designed to gain the opposite result

1098

Ignoring all, I continue to gaze—stare, to be exact
And that's enough to make her silly act retract

1099

To look at one you love as if you do not know her
Is part of the slow opening of love's shy door

1100

Then it becomes eye to eye, gaze to loving gaze
And words said unsaid fade into a distant haze

Chapter 111

THE EMBRACE

1101

This girl holds them all, all five senses, in her clasp
I see, hear, touch, scent and—taste with a gasp

1102

Illness and its cure are polar opposites, right?
This girl blinds me and then becomes the purpose of my sight

1103

In this creation of the Lotus-eyed, no grace
Can match the soft tenacity of her embrace

1104

She burns is all I know, she burns
Me up as I come in and as I retreat
She burns with yet another heat
She burns then soothes then burns in burning turns

1105

One has dreams one lives with, right?
Seen by day and known by night
Those dreams she braids feelingly
A flower vine tightly coiled to me

One also knows ambrosia, right?
But in her arms I know its scent, its sight
I feel its touch and a pulse I have not known
In each sleeping nerve of mine and in every bone

1107

When in her warm and warming clasp
A sense of being earthed I grasp
Of being there where I belong
And where I get for what I long

1108

The clasp is as tight as the love is true
And fastened thus lets no ill through

1109

Trust steps in where strife has tried to venture
All bruises heal all wounds congeal under love's rapture

1110

Love's classes kill!
When I think I'm done I'm not
And find I am a novice still
Before my begemmed despot

Chapter 112

HER BEAUTY

1111

There is the flower that shrinks when touched
This girl in her moods is even touchier
Nothing then pacifies her
One near-touch and watch the look it brings!

1112

This 'flower-like bloom' stuff is all wrong
Blooming blossoms to all belong!
I want her to be mine in bud, mine in bloom
Mine in ecstasy, mine in doom

1113

Her frame's soft, pearl-teeth tender
And a fragrance hovers about
Her shoulders slender ask me to hold her
While her eyes put me to rout

1114

The lily sees her, bends and rues
'With her around what is my use?'

1115

She rings her waist with touch-me-nots
Forgets to snip their stems
The wreaths alas become hard waistcoats
When they should've been soft hems

1116

The stars are in panic
Is this the moon or its mimic?
They ask each other in wonder
And not finding an answer, flounder

1117

As it swells and thins the moon its flaws reveals
But this moon, flawless, awes the show it steals

1118

And so no use have I, no use, for you, dear, dear moon
Go your way, I have another, morning, night and noon

1119

Besides, good moon, you're there for everyone, right?
You can't be mine, mine alone, for just my own night

1120

Softer than a swan's down or the touch-me-not
Are her feet that have me so besot

Chapter 113

LOVE'S SPECIAL EXCELLENCE

He

1121

The 'milk and honey' thing is overdone and nothing new
But what is one to do? The two do blend on her breath to form
nectar's dew

1122

This girl and I coming together in what could be called 'fluxion'
Is, plain and simple, an exhilaration

1123

Move over, eye-pupil, move over
So she whose pupil I am (as she is mine at times)
Can come where your light the moonbeam mimes
Be good, eye-pupil, make room, please, for her

1124

As she comes near, my lights come on
And as she goes, so they are gone!

1125

I forget and sigh, recall and smile and then forget again
But the sharp eyed one! *She* is lodged in my brain!

She

1126

He lives in my eyes
(This is no surprise)
I do not let them close
For he breathes in those

1127

In my eyes he lies
And with collyrium vies
So to put him out of doubt
The pigment now is out

1128

He says, 'We're one, you and I'
So foods that have fire

I now shun
I cannot have him burn
1129

If I as much as close my eyes and seem to be distrait
The townsfolk say, 'He's left her, the heartless ingrate'
1130

I know he's part of me and will always be
But the gossip-loving town says
'The wretch's fled, doubtless, to another country'
It so hurts, it does, the town's tattling ways

Chapter 114

THE ABANDONMENT OF RESERVE

He

1131

The palm-frond mimes a horse
A horse's mane its leaves
Riding it's the remorse
Custom decrees
So now forsaking all reserve
I will ride the horse of palm
Its duties observe
And keep the while my calm
1132

Leaving aside my shame, my ego's very sound
The horse of palm I'll mount
1133

I've had my pride, a skin thick as hide
But today I will the horse of palm ride
1134

My little raft of manly shame ready, now, blame to face
Love's great swell will overturn and lift me in embrace
1135

It is evening as I get there when her maid with a slender arm
That wears flowers brings the horse of palm

1136

I climb at midnight hour set for the horse of palm
Thinking, 'Is she angry with me and just acting calm?'

1137

The woman who, love-bound, does not mount
The horse of palm is worthy by any count

She

1138

We are discreet in our loving!
I hold tight its secrets in my soul
Like coppers in a beggar's bowl
But the nosey barge right in!

1139

And so what was quiet till now, almost a secret
Will wander out, open, in the public street

1140

My pains in love bystanders will never know
They'll mock me and at my discomfiture crow

Chapter 115

THE RUMOUR

He

1141

Rumours are an ill thing but can sometimes do good
My townsfolk's whispers are raising me to husbandhood

1142

Chatter's making her mine before the priests can
Make me hers in the state called 'wife and man'

1143

The town's seasoned gossipers are hastening us
Quite unwittingly to matrimonial status

1144

This rumour about us excites me and arouses
What I'll call 'love' knowing that word houses
A sense of virile power which can easily wilt
If townsfolk do not keep the rumour milled

The drinker gets drunk, drinks more the more drunk to get
I get caught making love, love the more to tangle in the net

She
1146

I saw him but once and that was enough to make rumours fly
Spreading like darkness in the moon-devouring dragon's sky
1147

I pine, my pining is a plant the town manures
By gossip and my mother's scolding waters; I pine
1148

My love all rumour will defy
That grease will never put out my fire
1149

I have known those saying, 'Do not fear'
Vanish after saying, 'I'm here'
I refuse absolutely to be taken
As weak or by cheap rumour be shaken
1150

I think rumours are in fact just as well
They'll make my love do what they tell

Chapter 116

THE SEPARATION UNENDURABLE

1151

Tell me if he says 'Go? Of course I won't!'
But if he says 'I'll soon be back,' don't tell me, don't!
1152

Waiting for his return was an unendurable torment
Now he's back, fear of his going haunts every moment
1153

He knows one day all bonds must sever
And so I discount his 'never' and 'ever'
1154

Fool I, to have believed when he said 'never'
Truant men are, by instinct and need, clever

1155

Help me, if you can, to keep him ever from parting
Once parted, there neither is nor can ever be returning

1156

If he could say to my face like that—'I go'
He's hard is no difficult thing to know

1157

As the bangle slipped, my bare arm warned me
He'll soon be gone to the gleeful arms of the sea

1158

Hard it is, very hard, to live where sour people dwell
Harder far from there to bid a loving one farewell

1159

Fire burns when you are anywhere near it
Love, when you are far from the cause of its heat

1160

Bearing it, not complaining, if not quite smiling too
Many live alone who should have been two

Chapter 117

COMPLAININGS

1161

My pain I want to hide
But a river bidden
To surge to a tide
Is not to be hidden

1162

I cannot hide my pain for pain is, after all, pain
But crying, 'Pain, pain!' is a shame I don't want to gain

1163

There is love, there is pain
Like two polar ends
Both in my soul remain
And can never be friends

1164

My love heaves like a breathless sea
But oh! for a boat that will ferry me

1165

When such is the grief from his love I get
What infernal pains will his rage beget?

1166

When love is, it is a seething ocean of joy
When pain is, it will your very soul destroy

1167

I am mid-sea in love with no shore in sight
In the very witching middle of the night

1168

All around me sleep a very deep sleep
While the night I, and me the night, company keep

1169

It is cruel of him to leave me this long
With sleepless nights becoming a thong

1170

If my eyes could go, as my soul does, to where he is
They would not have to swim in tears like this

Chapter 118

GRIEVING EYES

1171

My eyes showed him to me and said, 'All yours, to keep'
And now when he is away the same introducers weep

1172

Oh my eyes, my eyes, having spotted
Him for me, got me right besotted
And smarting now in their own brine
Want me to say, 'Stop crying!'

1173

Darting this way and that, these eyes of mine
Refuse to get their act together and turn off the brine

1174

They have wept themselves dry, they have, my poor silly eyes
The aquifer has no water left yet the more it tries

1175

They drag my pain into their seas
My eyes, and lose all sleep, all ease

1176

They have given me grief, my eyes, given me sorrow
Let them suffer, yes, suffer, now and every morrow

1177

Let them ache, let them smart, those eyes that spotted him
Let those eyes run dry that're now filled to the brim

1178

Who loved me once and does no more
My eyes want to see, his mind to know

1179

If they see him they'll forget sleep, if not they'll stay awake
In sleeplessness is their stake, their ache

1180

My eyes say it all, they do, in fact they drum it loud
Townsfolk know it all from that double thunder-cloud?

Chapter 119

THE PALLID HUE

1181

To his 'I must go', I said 'Do'
And authored my own loneliness
Covered now with a pallid hue
I must blame myself for the illness

1182

The climbing hue's his gift I say
And in such delusion waste away

1183

Where beauty was, now pallor is
And in dignity's place—this nameless *this*

His thoughts I praise, his words applaud
Why should I find my pallid hue so odd?

1185

There he goes, goes he, to the great deep blue
And here it comes, comes swiftly, my deep pallid hue

1186

Darkness waits for the lamp to end in smoke
To seize what was once the flame's domain
Cold pallor waits for his embrace to uncloak
And clasp what lies in love's terrain

1187

Coiled in his embrace I lay but when I moved a little, awhile
Cold pallor seized me in its bilious guile

1188

They fault me, they do, for my pallid hue
But none says it's wrong, it's bad, that he just upped and flew!

1189

Let me be pallid, sicklied, wan
But safe on his journey, stay my man

1190

Let me be called pallid or any old thing
But none should speak ill of my heart's king

Chapter 120

THE SOLITARY ANGUISH

1191

To love and to have the loved one that love return
Is to find the fruit one loves unhampered by its stone

1192

To love and to have the loved one with love respond
Mirrors the heavens giving rain to soothe our despond

1193

Love by the loved one returned alone
May say 'All the world's joys we share as one'

1194
All the world's love's just an empty urn
If with love the loved one doesn't love return

1195
If the one I love loves me not
What matters what else from the world I've got

1196
One-sided love's, well, just that—one sided
Love's love when to love both have decided

1197
If being mine and knowing me the love god
Does not see my pain, is it not very, very odd?

1198
If your loved one does not say, 'For you I crave'
And still you love him you can only be called brave

1199
What do I do—I know he cares not for me
Yet I find every word he utters a rhapsody

1200
Tell him how much it hurts that he does not care for me?
Forget it! I might as well drain then fill with tears the sea

Chapter 121

MEMORIES

He
1201
I have to but think of her and I go on a high
A high with which sweet toddy cannot vie

1202
I have to but think of her and there ring a hundred happy bells
Love, ah, love is just something else

She
1203
Just as it was coming, the sneeze, it changed its mind
So was he about to think of me only another one to find?

1204

Don't ask me why but in my heart he lives
The question is do I in his

1205

From his heart he stops me with a stern, 'No admittance!'
But in mine stays put, my shameless ex and once

1206

He's left, I live, it's strange and only I know how I do
Memory holds my hand saying, 'I'm here with you'

1207

Remembering, I burn
What would forgetting earn?

1208

My ceaseless thinking of him does not ruffle him
This is a gift that fills my cup of love to its brim

1209

My life slips ways as I brood, hurt, so alone
On one who once said to me, 'We are but one'

1210

Set not, moon, set not that by your argent light
I will yet see him who has turned my day to endless night

Chapter 122

VISIONS OF THE NIGHT

1211

My love sends a message through his herald—I rejoice!
I'm giddy with the gladness of a thousand joys
But is this a vision I'm dreaming this night?
I should make a feast for the herald but, ayyaiyo, he's only a sprite

1212

I want to will a dream in which my love must hear
The story of my pain and its price that he must bear

1213

I do not see him in life trying kindness to give
But I do, in dreams, and so manage to live

1214

The joys he does not give me when I'm awake
I get dreams, for my imagined joy, to make

1215

My dreams, in every small detail, can make, remake
The joys that he and I knew when our love was awake

1216

And if, a very big if, there was to be no wake
My love would never leave my side another to take

1217

Uncaring in 'real life' if that's the horror's name
In my dream's innocent hours too he's just the same

1218

Sleeping, to his breast he holds me
Waking, wants my heart to see

1219

If in your dream you do not see your beloved
You will, when awake, grieve for the unloved

1220

Townsfolk, seeing me, say he's left me in misery
They don't see him in my dreams tell another story

Chapter 123

LAMENTS IN THE EVENING

1221

For one whose life's lost its meaning
Evening's no gentle angel thing!

1222

Your eyes are sad, Evening mine, and as I do, you moan
Has a cruel one left you too utterly alone?

1223

As you settle, my Evening, on grass you lay the dew
And unknown to you my anguish you renew

1224

Evening's gentle cruelty
Makes it a killer for me

1225

What ill have I caused you, Evening, that you should give me such
grief?
And what good have I done to Morning that it brings me such
relief?

1226

That evening could be so hard I could not have known
Till one morning I saw that he was gone

1227

Grief's a bud at morning, an opening flower by day
But by evening, full-blown, it has set its cruel sway

1228

The cowherd's gentle flute tells all, 'Evening has come'
To me it trills the disaster my life has now become

1229

If evening drowned the town in gloom as it drowns me
There would be heard for far and long a wail of agony

1230

When my darkened soul thinks of his love of gain
It will not be able to survive sheer destitution's pain

Chapter 124

WASTING AWAY

She

1231

The eyes grow dim like flowers long dead
Thinking of him who from my home has fled

1232

My lustreless eyes speak without moving
Of him who remains so utterly unloving

1234

When he left, my armlets, bereft, from their strong hold
On my now wasting arms slipped and on to the ground rolled

1235

My wasted arms and armlets forlorn bear testimony
To the cruel one's contempt for the codes of matrimony

1236

And yet I grieve to hear him rebuked as cruel
Merely because of the slipping armlet rule

1237

Should my heart to the cruel one complain
Of my armlets' fate it will only gain but more pain

He

1238

When I once turned from her bejewelled embrace
The glow on her forehead vanished without trace

1239

Again she was angry with me when I left a space
No wider than a breath in our passionate embrace

1240

Her dimming eyes now felt sad
Her quivering brows had gone so mad

Chapter 125

SOLILOQUY

She

1241

Prescribe, my heart, dispense, please, a quick relief
To cure me of my grief

1242

Go you on now, my heart, you're a fool to grieve
Over one whose life's business it is to deceive

1243

Your pining's a waste, my heart, a total waste of time
For he knows no pity and would hold compassion a crime

1244

You want to go to him, I know
So go, but take my eyes when you go
For crying, 'I want to see him, I want to'
They are eating me up so

Tell me, my heart, can I give up on him—should I—
Even though he cares not if I live or die?

1246

When he returns, I know, my heart, you won't protest
Your anger's just an act, a stance, at best

1247

Give up one or other: your lust for him or your modest-modest act
I cannot take any more this double life you've so skilfully hacked

1248

Pitiless you call him, heartless, merciless and many other 'less'es
Yet behind him you'll run though you know the mess your life is

1249

When you know he lives in you, my heart
Why looking for him here and there do you dart?

1250

If any longer, even one moment longer, I wallow in self-pity
For his forsaking me I'll lose what little is left of my dignity

Chapter 126

RESERVE OVERCOME

1251

I had fastened love's door with the iron bolts of reserve
But now with love's own axe I've broken it open to love

1252

This thing called love neither has nor gives rest
In the midnight hour it puts me to the severest test

1253

It cannot be held back and it cannot be hid
Achoos! cannot come under reserve's lid

1254

I thought in modesty I had no equal
But love comes tearing through the veil

1255

To crave for him who cares not for you
Is an indignity love makes you endure

1256
It is a kind of grace I do believe
For him who hates you to grieve
1257
Modest reserve will have no role to play
When with love all my doubting he comes to slay
1258
He words his words with words' wily ways
And a woman's disbelieving heart with sounds, slays
1259
I'd said I'll have nothing to do with one so stone-hearted
But when he held me in a hard rock-like embrace, I just melted
1260
To say, 'I'll stay away from him whose heart is hard'
Is to say a boiling pot will not dissolve melting lard

Chapter 127

MUTUAL DESIRE

She
1261
My eyes have gone hazy scouring the path he'll come on
My fingers ache marking on the wall the days he's been gone
1262
To 'forget him', as you suggest, may seem quite easy
If I do, every jewel will slide off—like crazy
1263
He's gone to win the war with no other thought in mind
And with no thought but of him, left me behind
1264
As my heart tells me to climb a tall tree
To watch him arrive, desire climbs throbbing in me
1265
The instant, the very instant, I see him return
Pallor will flee my limbs, my skin cease to burn

1266

The day he returns home, oh, the day he comes back to me
Will be ambrosial and will see all grief, sorrow, lament, flee

1267

Should I, when he's home, scold him for looking all grim
Or hold him or let him hold me and melting, melt him

1268

May he, victorious, share victory's gains with grace
Come home tonight to a feast of joy and to my embrace

1269

For those who wait for the loved one's return
From wanderings far, one day is as long as seven

He

1270

My return home is worthless, my victory no reward
If I find her, my life, my soul, lying at home, a shard

Chapter 128

READING MORE SIGNS

He

1271

I do not know of what but your eyes a complaint did lodge
I saw that as a sign though you tried my eyes to dodge

1272

Her comely looks are made richer
By her modest and restrained nature
Her shoulders—ah—like the bamboo curve
Do I one precious as her deserve?

1273

Just as in a necklace hides a thread that holds the beads
In her beauty lies a string of thoughts no one reads

1274

As in a bud about to open there breathes a subtle fragrance
So this girl's faint flickering smile hides a delicious nuance

1275

Her ways that sometimes seem like wiles
Transform my cares to smiles

She

1276

His heart was heavy, I saw, as he held me to leave
That was a sign, I know, that I was going to grieve

1277

The armlets, the armlets, they know and say it all
Slipping as they did, they presaged my reunion's fall

1278

He left me but yesterday but my limbs
Say that to them, like seven days it seems

Her Companion

1279

She looked at her arms, my lady did, and at her slipping amulets
She looked at her feet, she did, and looked sad as sad sunsets

He

1280

It is a ruse, a trick, I'd say, to use the eyes to plead
It is a woman's instrument and is her very creed

Chapter 129

DESIRE FOR REUNION

She

1281

A state of sweet intoxication by its very thought
Is not by foaming toddy but by upcoming love brought

1282

When love rises and stands as a palm tree, tall
Distrust shrinks to less than the millet small

1283

His heaving ocean-like ego being, to him, is all that matters
I, his lover, am just about there in the still backwaters

1284

I went resolved, my friend, to show him utter contempt
But when I stood there, face to face, all that—just went!

1285

The eye does not see the liner draw its black rimming line
As I don't see my love's faults when his eyes pierce mine

1286

When he stands before me he, well, just glows
And every fault of his dissolves into thin air
But how I hate—and berate—his godawful flaws
When I am alone and he, as always, is just not there

1287

I made up an angry scene and arrived all flame and fury
Like when rescue is at hand, one feigns a drowning story

1288

Toddy's bad, I know, it does real harm, but how it attracts!
Stealer of my heart, usurper, you, your strong chest, it distracts!

He

1289

Love's tender, as tender, as a slow-opening flower
Not many know—the less perhaps the better!—its secret hour

1290

Her eyes blaze when anger tells its hard tale
But as love steals in, they turn to the softest pastel

Chapter 130

EXPOSTULATION WITH ONESELF

She

1291

His heart, you see, he owns as his and his alone
Why cannot you, my heart, be mine alone to own?

1292

He is distant from you, cold, remote, right, my heart?
Now you go on do the same, the very same, on your part

When you hanker after him, my heart, though he has forsaken me
You prove the old belief that failures—like me—have no company

There's no point baring my heart, for my heart has its own
Heart which now belongs to him and has left me forlorn

I fear I'll lose him or, finding him, will lose him again
So pain endures and relief, if any comes at all, is in vain

My lonely heart devours itself being so alone
With no one but itself its own fate to bemoan

Can there be worse shame
Than my heart saying 'No'
When I tell it my aim
Is to let his memory go?

My heart rebukes me as I count his faults: one, two, three...
And says I should count his virtues that nudge infinity...

I wonder who if anyone will give me relief
When my own heart scoffs at my grief?

What do I take as mine if when I'm in lonely pain
My heart, my very own heart, treats me with disdain?

Chapter 131

POUTING

1301

Stay your hand awhile from heeding his call
Enchain him, love, in your unyielding thrall

1302

But hold the holding back for just that long, no longer
Salt the tongue must savour just so and no stronger

1303

He must be made to languish yet not lose face
The human in the heartless can do with an embrace
1304
To be unavailing to one who sulks abashed
Is to have a plant, at its very tender root, slashed
1305
Affected coyness in flower-like eyes has its allure
Even so-called good men are drawn to its lure
1306
Ripened fruit is the love that knows no strife
Raw it is and raw remains, that with discord rife
1307
Strife leads to pain, add to this doubt which too is pain:
Will we ever make up and be as one again?
1308
No good comes from crying, 'He's cold', no good whatsoever
If there's not one caring soul around to tell him, 'You must listen
to her'
1309
Water is a doubled joy by the cooling grove
As is being together in the twosome shade of love
1310
In my heart to yet think of one who grief-stricken has left me
Is proof of a love that is pure and innocent—of history

Chapter 132

FEIGNED ANGER

She
131

Glad of eye, you traitor you, winning all women with your smile
I recoil from the very thought of embracing one so vile
1312
You sneezed, I know, on purpose just to hear me say, 'Long live!'
Don't think me a fool who can't see through your mischief

He

1313
When I sported flowers one day a tempest was unloosed
Of faithlessness and disloyalty I stood in the dock, accused

1314
Fool I am, such a fool! 'I love you,' I said, 'more than anyone else'
'Else?' she screamed, 'who else, tell me, tell me, who is else?'

1315
Fool that I am I said, '*This* life' vowing love to quell her fears
'*This* life, right?' she said, 'not every life?' and burst into tears

1316
When, double, treble fool, I said, 'I remember you every day'
'So you forget me, right, to have to *remember*... leave me, go away!'

1317
What *does* one do?
Like anyone else I sneezed
'Bless you!' she said, 'bless you'
But then her forehead creased
'Which woman, tell me, which woman
Is it that's brought your sneezing on?'
What does one do
To make this girl trust you?

1318
Going by last time, I checked my sneeze
When I heard, 'Who on your mind does weigh
That you can't do as you please?'
Impossible's all I say

1319
I calmed her down, said, 'Now, now, don't be silly'
Only to hear, 'But are you to all just as friendly?'

1320
Finally, I thought I'd stay quiet and gaze into her face
'Don't fool me,' she goes, 'I see in your eyes *her* trace'

Chapter 133

PLEASURES OF TEMPORARY VARIANCE

She

1321

He is quite, quite free of the usual manly fault
But his very sweetness makes my suspicion vault

1322

Feigned anger has its uses
It causes for a while some pain
But when love to tedium loses
Acting hurt revives it again

1323

No bliss can be more blissful than when two hearts
Beat like earth and water so a pulse of new life starts

1324

Anger put on crumbles at a touch—the merest touch
Of a close-shared love's soul-scorching search

He

1325

For the joy I want from love's warm clasp
I must for a while be free from its grasp

1326

To take in what you eat feels good, to savour it more fun
Union is, what shall I say...but what precedes it is heaven

1327

When they quarrel, as they do, one that holds the other yields
But when the two make up, the yielder success wields

1328

The game of love in feigned anger played ended in a clasp
The beauty of which I want forever to hold in my grateful grasp

1329

Girl mine, do not yield to me, do not, I say, do not
Let our feigned game cool this night that's so, ah, so very hot

1330

Acting coy, coy acting, has added to love that thing
Which makes me want her to me and me to her cling

ACKNOWLEDGEMENTS

My first word of thanks has to go to David Davidar for suggesting this venture into a land that would have otherwise remained, for me, a distant Antarctica of frozen wisdoms.

And to Kalakshetra, Chennai, for giving me on a long loan its rare copy of Rev. G. U. Pope's *Sacred Kurral*; to Sri K. V. Ramanathan and Sri K. N. Varadarajan for my first ever conversations on the text and for suggesting that I read *Tirukkural: Puthiya Urai* (Uyirmai Pathippakam, Chennai, 1995) by 'Sujata' Rangarajan.

I owe B. Mathivanan, Professor of Tamil at the Bharatidasan University, Tiruchirappalli and A. R. Venkatachalapathy, Professor at the Madras Institute of Development Studies, Chennai, deepest thanks for the benefaction of thought-sharing on the couplets and for the most invaluable comments on my grasp of them. Such merit as my renderings may possess are ascribable to my discussions with those two scholars while, needless to say, their demerits remain my exclusive domain. I also owe them thanks for placing in my hands the following books:

On Translating Tirukkural (International Institute of Tamil Studies, Chennai, 2001) by Dr V. Ramasamy;

Tirukkural: Arattuppal, Porutpal, Kamattupal–Mulamum, Parimelazhahar Uraiyum (Uma Pathippakam, Chennai) compiled with commentaries by V. M. Gopalakrishnamachariar;

Tiruvalluvar Aruliya Tirukkural (Meenakshi Puthaga Nilayam, Madurai, 2007) by Tamizhannal;

Tirukkuralum Periyarum (Periyar Suyamariyadai Prachara Niruvanam, Chennai, 1983);

Tirukkuratsolladaivu (Tennindia Tamizh Sangam, Chennai, 2002) by Swami Velayudham.

Professor Venkatachalapathy, who is currently working on a biography of Periyar E. V. Ramasami, acquainted me with that remarkable thinker's work *Penn Yen Adimaiyaanaal?*, which has been translated with great felicity by the author Meena Kandasamy and published in 2007 as *Why Women Were Enslaved* by the Periyar Self Respect Propaganda Institution, Chennai. To Justice Prabha

Sridevan (Retd.) and S. T. Baskaran, I owe thanks for enabling me to understand Periyar's observations better.

Mandayam Venkatesh of San Diego procured for me a new edition of *Tirukkural: The Holy Scripture* published by the International Tamil Language Foundation, Illinois, USA in the likeness of a gilt-edged Holy Bible, complete with rounded corners and a string bookmark. The incorporation in it of P. S. Sundaram's English rendering of the 1,330 couplets was of much use to me. G. Sundar, Director of the Roja Muthiah Research Library, Chennai, very kindly provided me with a photocopy of Rajagopalachari's 1937 rendering published by Rochouse & Sons, Esplanade, Madras, going by a telltale title: *The Second Book of Kural: A Selection from the Old Tamil Code for Princes, Statesmen and Men of Affairs.*

During the months that I was working on the *Kural*, I was Senior Fellow at the Shiv Nadar University's Centre for Public Affairs and Critical Theory (C-PACT). The support that fellowship gave was as timely as it was generous. I acknowledge it here with sincere appreciation and gratitude.

It is my pleasant duty to acknowledge the most valuable editorial guidance I received from Aleph's editors, Pujitha Krishnan and Aienla Ozukum, in the final stages of the translation.